GROWTH

MINDSET

UNIVERSITY

LEARN ANYTHING

TAKE CONTROL OF YOUR LIFE

FULFILL YOUR VISION OF SUCCESS

JORDAN PARIS

Internet addresses and chapter resources provided in this book were accurate at the time of print.

© 2018 by Jordan Paris

Cover Photo: Tanner Crooks

Cover Design: Jordan Paris

ISBN: 1-7323079-0-3
ISBN-13: 978-1-7323079-0-2

To my parents,
Scot and Maria Paris.
Thank you for giving me the unconditional love and support
that has enabled me to chase my dreams. I love you.

CONTENTS

"Intellectual growth should commence at birth and cease only at death."

—Albert Einstein

INTRODUCTION

"It's what you learn after you know it all that counts."
—John Wooden

GROWTH

MINDSET

UNIVERSITY

I know nothing.

If we're honest, we'll admit that none of us really know what we're doing. We're all just winging it. Some of us think we're hot stuff and that we have it all figured out, but the reality is that none of us are hot stuff and none of us have it all figured out.

I used to hate people. I thought my intelligence was fixed. I thought that Listerine mouthwash was just a sort of minty Kool-Aid, so I would sneak into my parents' bathroom when I was a young boy to drink it every day. I thought I would be a kid forever merely because I *was* a kid at the time. I thought bread was a health food. I thought I was right and everyone else was wrong. I felt that I knew it all and that I would be set for life with the knowledge I already had.

I was wrong.

So wrong.

For much of my life, I walked around with a full glass in the sense that I knew it all. There's great danger in that because when the glass is full, it cannot be filled with anything new. I was closed-minded, and it cut me off from becoming the best version of myself. The worst part is that the contents of my glass were full of ignorance. I'm always wrong and I probably always will be wrong, but the power of continual growth and development allows me to improve upon my beliefs and assumptions continually. Continual growth and development is where the joy is, where the fulfillment is, and where life happens. Life is a learning experience. I live to learn and grow to give. That's pretty fun for me.

I learned that every person could be beautiful if I just got to know them by sparking a conversation that goes beyond the surface. I realized that I love people. I learned that intelligence was merely a state of mind that I had considerable control over. By the time I was a teenager, I had learned that Listerine was dangerous to drink when I finally realized that the bottle said, "In case of accidental ingestion contact a poison control center or doctor immediately." I learned that I wouldn't be a kid forever and that adulthood would come fast and furious. I learned that bread makes you weak, fat, and tired. I learned that everyone thinks they are right. I learned that if I was going to do anything meaningful with my life, then I was going to have to commit to continual growth and development, and I would be a failure if I became complacent at any point.

Oddly enough, it seems that the more I learn, I realize just how little I actually know about the world. But I find peace in knowing that I don't know. It makes learning a joyful experience. Happiness comes from growing, and confidence comes from learning. Knowing that I don't know everything allows me to laugh at myself, it allows me to grow each day, it allows me to find joy from new challenges each day, which enables me to foster a deep love for life.

WHAT'S YOUR DEAL, JORDAN?

Truthfully, my upbringing wasn't anything out of the ordinary and my story isn't all that crazy either. The short version goes like this: I was depressed. I hated everything. Life sucked all the way around because I made it so; I did it to myself. Nevertheless, I ended up using my trouble as transportation that put me on a path of continual growth and development, and consequently, a life full of joy. The more detailed version is below.

My Story began 20 years ago, in a small town outside of Philadelphia called Collegeville. I was the first born of three children. My father worked long hours as a general surgeon and my mother was a nurse (you can guess how they met). I was relatively privileged, but that didn't exempt me from experiencing challenges.

In my younger years, my life revolved around baseball and I was usually the class clown every year. In fact, I even won the class clown award at the end of fourth grade. This humor lasted another few years until high school came along.

High school started off well, at least for the first month. My grades were pretty good, I didn't have any major stressors in my life, and I even started dating a girl I liked from class. I was young and naïve, so I became attached to her relatively quickly, putting all of my happiness into one basket, and as the record has it, she broke up with me two days before the homecoming dance for that exact reason.

Like many naïve and sensitive 15-year-olds who get dumped, I thought the world was coming to an end. I was crushed because I put my happiness into her hands, and she dropped it. Woops.

I remember going home from school that day, running right past my mom and locking myself in my room. The tears started coming, and they didn't stop until the moment I fell asleep that night.

From that day on, everything seemed to spiral out of control. That same week, I got terrible acne for the first time in my life. My grades slipped. My performance in baseball slipped. All the friends I had made as the class clown in previous years seemed to leave me. Walking through the halls at school, I felt like nobody liked me and I cried just about

3

every day. I felt diminished. There were some days I didn't even say a word.

I let one singular event break me down to my core.

Now, I know you're thinking about how silly it is that I'm starting off by telling you some story about a girl breaking up with me. I feel even sillier writing it, so I understand that.

But I'm telling you this story to illustrate that everything in life begins and ends in the mind because in the same way I *decided* to allow one unrelated event to affect everything in my life, I *decided* to pick up the pieces years later.

In the grand scheme of things, that event shouldn't have affected me the way it did, but I didn't know any better, so I lived depressed for most of my high school career and lost all of my friends. I never went to homecoming. I never went to prom. I told myself that nobody liked me or nobody cared about me and that became the most disempowering self-fulfilling prophecy of my entire life.

Looking back, I wish I made the most of my high school experience but I just didn't do that. Instead, I *decided* to host my own pity party.

My perspective of life was nearsighted, and I only saw the battles I was currently fighting with no vision of a brighter future. I got caught up in the *current*. It was all about *current* events, *current* problems, *current* fears. That *current* sucked me up and I ended up going with that *flow* for many years, letting it take me wherever.

My mindset was limited. I thought I was only average, I complained of not being as smart as my father, who graduated at the top of his classes, and my brother who routinely got 100's in his classes without even trying. I spent all this time wishing my circumstances were different without realizing that if things were going to change, *I* had to change and I had to *decide* to do so.

The Day That Turned My Life Around

My mother and I were in a meeting with the school guidance counselor talking about some of my troubles, mostly about my bad grades, and what we could do about it all. At this point, I'd been depressed for a while. Toward the end of the meeting, my mother said something that has stuck with me since that day and has played a significant role in shaping my mindset. She said to the counselor, "Well, Jordan is a *sponge*, so I know he can do it; he just has to apply himself."

What a profound statement!

As if it were magic, I applied myself more in school, believing I was a *sponge* that could soak up all knowledge and learn any skill. I went from borderline "B" student to consistent "A" student. I ended up getting into all five schools I applied to when in the past I thought I would have to settle for community college. Then I applied myself in a little something called personal development. Little did I know, the order of my entire life was about to explode into change.

In my junior year of high school, an Uncle of mine demonstrated an act of pure grace when he gifted me a book that changed my life, *Awaken the Giant Within* by Tony Robbins. I thought I was a sponge, and I was hungry for massive change in my life, so I read this book like there was no tomorrow. I did all the exercises in the book. I even wrote *40 full pages of notes* on it, which I still review every few months. By the time I finished reading this book, my whole philosophy of life had changed. I knew what I had to do; knowing full well that I had the capacity to take control of my life, I had to commit to my absolute best self through constant and never-ending improvement, and **I had to make sure my actions aligned with my affirmations.** Then I read another book, and another, and another, and I never looked back. I kept learning.

5

I kept growing. I kept absorbing, like a sponge. I was free to learn anything I wanted. I soon realized that there is a book, podcast, video, mentor, or role model to learn just about anything or to build any skill. With that, I became obsessed with creating my reality. I was hooked on learning and developing new skills. It's what got me out of bed in the morning. *I was a sponge.* When I started applying myself and embracing the challenge of becoming my best self, my depression faded because my focus shifted. My whole mindset shifted. Tony Robbins said, "Where focus goes, energy flows." That was incredibly true for me. I went from having a limited mindset to having a *growth mindset*, which we'll go into detail about later. The lens through which I saw the world went from nearsighted to having a metaphorical 20/20 vision, meaning I was focused on short-term goals and challenges while simultaneously creating my vision of the future with long-term goals. My mind was free to romp as it never had before. The best part was that Instead of hitting snooze every morning, I began springing out of bed with excitement. In fact, some nights I can hardly fall asleep because I'm so excited for life and whatever new skill I am currently mastering! I went from hopelessly average, lonely, and miserable to doing things in my career that I am incredibly proud of, having an abundance of friends, and ultimately creating a life that (frankly) sucks less than others'.

I credit everything to learning and the power of a growth mindset. **I believe that learning is our superpower and a growth mindset is the engine that drives our levels of joy and fulfillment in life.**

THE BASELINE

"Formal education will make you a living; self-education will make you a fortune."
—Jim Rohn

Traditional schooling has never been enough for me. While I do believe a degree is necessary, there are essential skills that college does not teach extensively enough, if at all. I never learned the art of holding a conversation, the science of people, how to network, how to form deep and meaningful relationships, empowering thought patterns and how to think in general, what sets successful people apart, how to live joyfully, how to maximize my potential, how to *develop* my unique inspiration and gifts, how to utilize failure to my advantage, how to eat right, how to turn thoughts into action, how to love and respect myself, how to manage and accept my emotions, how to cultivate gratitude so that I could not be an ungrateful prick, how to not be so entitled, how to build confidence and find my true identity, how to negotiate, how to invest, how to create a clear vision, how to find balance in my life, the power of personal development, how to be a leader, how to influence people, how to create a life I could be proud of, and how to do anything other than work in the corporate world for 50 years then retire. I didn't learn any of that.

Instead, I learned math, science, reading, writing, and how to figure out the exact degree of an angle at which a ladder leans against a wall. Most of this is useful, depending upon your career, but this is the education baseline. I realized that if I was ever going to do anything meaningful and beyond the ordinary, I was going to have to seek out other resources, like books, mentors, interviews, and the like. I was going to have to learn on my own, voluntarily (the way learning should be), and that's precisely what I did. I took it upon myself. I enrolled in the University of Life.

ENROLLING IN THE UNIVERSITY OF LIFE

"Learning is the beginning of wealth. Learning is the beginning of health. Learning is the beginning of spirituality. Searching and learning is where the miracle process all begins."
—Jim Rohn

I've become a student of health, wealth, happiness, fulfillment, and prosperities of all kind, and by doing so, I've raised my baseline for happiness, fulfillment, and other prosperities. In my studies over the years, I've found that I'm not alone in my commitment to lifelong learning in the name of fulfillment; Many of the most successful *and* fulfilled human beings on this great planet, have a common denominator among them: They have harnessed their superpower that is learning, and it is the philosophy of a growth mindset that drives it all. It is no coincidence that these people are as unique, successful and fulfilled as they are. **Most of what these extraordinary people have achieved didn't happen by chance. They haven't been walking through life with their fingers crossed, merely hoping things would go their way. Instead, they think prosperous thoughts and have a set of guiding principles that support their philosophy. Successful thoughts breed success. Prosperous thoughts breed prosperity. Happy thoughts breed happiness. Guiding principles produce outstanding results.**

Many people only see the successful results and call it *chance* or *luck*. What they don't understand are the effort and the process. They only see the car, not the thousands of moving parts that went into the making of the car. They only see and judge results, and in doing so, they fail to capitalize on their own power of thought to become the best versions of themselves. Behind every successful person are thoughts of success. Behind every happy person is happy thoughts. Behind every intelligent person is intelligent thoughts. Behind every healthy person is healthy thoughts. Behind every rich person is rich thoughts. In the same way, behind every depressed person is depressing thoughts. Behind every selfish person is selfish thoughts. Behind every poor person is poor thoughts. **As we think, we are.**

We may not be able to control our circumstances entirely, but we can always consciously direct our thoughts and master our minds, which indirectly shapes our circumstances.

"We are what we think. All that we are arises with our thoughts. With our thoughts, we make our world."
—The Buddha

The tragedy of today is that men and women across the world are desperate to improve their lives, yet they aren't willing to improve themselves. They aren't willing to develop new skills. They aren't willing to learn. They aren't willing to improve their thought patterns. They aren't willing to put in an effort that surpasses the minimum. So, they get "stuck". How many times have you heard someone say that they feel "stuck"?

Now, I don't claim to be an expert of any sort. Instead, **I'm a student of life,** just like you, and these are my observations. I continually look to my teachers for guidance. Lifestyle is never a one size fits all; what is true for me may not be true for you, and that's ok because coming to understand a wide-ranging spectrum of different perspectives is precisely what leads to wisdom. Even the perspective that is opposite of our own has incredible value, if not more so than any other perspective.

In any case, we should all be students of life. Instead of trying to just get through the day, we should strive to get *from* the day. Learn *from* each day. Learn *from* each experience; **Become a sponge, soak everything up and you will transform not only your life, but your partner's life, your family's life, and your friends' lives. If you improve, then your life will improve. When you walk around with the attitude that your results are your responsibility, there is no glass ceiling you cannot break.**

A FULFILLING PATH

Too often, people will settle for being hopelessly average even though they are more than capable of doing something remarkable in their lives. The sad part is that people don't do this because they think they have to, but instead because nobody showed them that there is a better way, that a more fulfilling path exists.

With this book, it is my goal not to be the visionary that knows it all and is frustrated that nobody else understands, but to be the guide that shows the way of a more empowering path, thus allowing for the possibility of that path to be traveled. If my path rings true for you, that's fantastic, but if not, then at least you gained a valuable new perspective. My fulfilling path is about cultivating a growth mindset, which can be broken down into 12, needle-moving core principles that we will discuss at length in each chapter of this book. With that being said, I am merely your guide. Some principles may work for you and others may not. Study and act on the ones that make the most sense for you. If they change your life, congratulate yourself, not me because I can only plant seeds of greatness in you, I cannot water them; that is up to you, dear reader.

1. **The Growth Mindset** - Those with a growth mindset

believe that if they don't know something, they can surely learn it and master it. They are creators, not victims, of their reality and masters of their ship. A growth mindset leads to prosperities of all kind.

2. **Feed the mind or fall behind** – In an everchanging world, complacency kills no matter how great we are, how old we are, or how wise we are. For this reason, knowledge is not something that accumulates and remains forever; it's use it or lose it. And the ones who think they know it all have no room to grow, no room to evolve. Further, businesses have failed and entire species have become extinct due to an inability to evolve. We must be lifelong learners if we wish to enjoy a prosperous life over the long-term.

3. **Know why** – Establishing a clear vision and reason for why we do what we do enables us to live with excitement. Being able to articulate this allows for the possibility of enrolling others in our vision. When we don't know why we do what we do, how is anyone else supposed to know? And why would they care?

4. **Invest in yourself** – The best investment we can make is an investment in ourselves. We must invest our time and energy into learning the skills we need to advance our vision of the world and our best self's place in it.

5. **Questions are the answer** – Habitually asking ourselves quality questions results in a high-quality life, and vice versa.

6. **Trouble is transportation** – We all go through times of difficulty. But the same thing can happen to two different people, and one person will interpret the meaning one way and go down a specific path, while

the other person will interpret the meaning a different way and go down the opposite path. Those with a growth mindset trust that any trouble is the transportation that delivers them to their next victory.

7. **Awaken your potential** - Overcome your fears and get after your dreams *today*. You don't need the weather to change, you don't need your upbringing to change, you don't need your luck to change, you don't need any circumstance to change for you to become your best self.

8. **Don't make a living, design a life** - Designing a beautiful life is all about making plans. If you want good health, make a plan to be healthy. If you want wealth, make a plan to be wealthy. If you want good relationships, make a plan to have good relationships. If you want to become a great public speaker, make a plan to become a great public speaker. If you want a prosperous business, make a business plan. If you want to be intelligent, make a study plan. If you want to be influential, make an influence plan. If you want to be happy, make a plan to be happy. Prosperities of all kind can be yours with a simple plan. The best part is that we don't have to be healthy to start a plan to be healthy, we don't have to be wealthy to start a plan to be wealthy, and so on. Decide on what you want and make a strategic plan to get there. What are you planning on?

9. **Grow to give** - The whole point of growing is to give because it adds meaning to our lives.

10. **Together is better** - If you have the chance to do terrific things in your life (you do), take someone with you. Partners help us level up in specific skills, and

they further add to the meaning of our lives.

11. **Take responsibility for your results** – There is no failure, only results, and the most significant sign of maturity is taking responsibility for those results.

12. **Live Impactfully** – To make an impact, we must define what making an impact means to us. Once we gain clarity of the impact we want to make, only then can we make our impact and leave a legacy.

This book is the result (to this point) of my learning experiences from life, daily reading, and my network of teachers and mentors. Throughout our studies, we will discover the thought patterns necessary to become your best self by planting seeds of greatness within you. **Our minds are merely gardens, and if we water our seeds of greatness, they will surely bloom, bringing forth sweet fruit in the form of prosperity.**

This book is divided into three phases, each signifying essential steps along the fulfilling path. In phase one, we will learn to **explore** the abundance of resources available to us, and the possibilities in this fantastic world. In phase two, we will learn to **create** our own reality. In phase 3, we will learn to **inspire** those around us by giving back, among other practices.

I understand I'm quite young, but I don't believe age is always accurate in determining the value one possesses to the give to the world. In fact, I have a 15-year-old client that is far more intelligent than I am, so I always make sure I learn from him as much as possible in the time we spend together.

And since you've made it this far, I want to acknowledge and thank you for trusting the process and having faith in the value I can offer you; I promise you won't regret taking the time to read this.

All I ask is that you read carefully and with openness. Increase your imagination, wit, heal your emotional pain, and in doing so, become the creator of your reality, the author of your story, and the master of your dreams.

Most importantly take all the ideas in, entertain them, but ensure your actions are the product of your own conclusions. You must consider how to apply these ideas and principles to your own life, or not. I can't be happy for you. And don't ever let someone be the co-author of your story. *You* are the author, my friend.

Let us also keep in mind that knowledge is only potential power; *Action is power.*

> *"If [more] information was the answer, then we'd all be billionaires with perfect abs."*
> —Derek Sivers

> *"Education without application is just entertainment."*
> —Tim Sanders

Extra Credit: Accompanying chapter resources for this book can be found at JordanParisHealth.com/gmu-backpack.

EXPLORE

"Don't exist. Live.
Get out, explore. Thrive.
Challenge authority. Challenge yourself.
Evolve. Change forever.
Become who you say you always will. Keep
moving. Don't stop. Start the revolution.
Become a freedom fighter. Become a
superhero. Just because everyone doesn't
know your name doesn't mean you don't
matter."
—Brian Krans

CHAPTER 1

THE GROWTH MINDSET

"Becoming is better than being."
—Carol S. Dweck

GROWTH

MINDSET

UNIVERSITY

It was my sophomore year of high school. I was in biology class, which I had bright and early every morning. It was a pretty tough class for me, especially considering the fact I didn't study for anything.

As usual, we were at the lab tables doing group work. I just sat there and depended on the rest of my group to do all the work, also per usual. As I sat there, a wide range of thoughts ran through my head.

"I wonder if I'll get a B or a C this semester."

"Who can I get the homework from tonight?"

"I wish I was smarter."

"How can I just 'get by'?"

"I wonder if my grades will be good enough to go away to college."

"I hope so."

"I hope things change."

"I wonder if I'll ever make good money."

"I hope I'll be rich, but it's whatever."

"When will I ever take the gym seriously?"

"I'm too skinny."

"I don't think I'll ever be happy."

"Will I ever have friends?"

"Will I ever find a partner?"

"Gosh, whatever."

"I can't wait for the day to be over."

These were my thoughts just about every single day. They

were disempowering and weak. My mindset sucked. All I did was *hope*, which got me nowhere.

I walked through life with my fingers crossed, merely hoping things would work out but never doing anything about it. I was only ever willing to do the bare minimum and I was "fine" settling for much less than my best. I thought my intelligence was at a fixed point and it became a self-fulfilling prophecy, as I wallowed in mediocrity for years.

I was unhappy with many different things but neglected to do anything about them. I was leaving everything in life to chance, not realizing that if things were going to change, I had to change. I had to make a decision to change and reinforce it with action. If I could have explored the great resources the world has to offer, I could have created my own reality and inspired the others to do the same.

But again, I had no idea that this fulfilling path was able to be taken because I simply had no concept of it. Nobody ever showed me this path existed.

Far too many people walk around with this limited mindset. Often, they try to "just get through the day." Quite frankly, those are the people that get to the end of life and say, "thank God it's over." This disempowering path was undoubtedly the one I was hurtling down with my limited mindset.

This path isn't the only option. I'm here to tell you there's a better way. And even if you already know there is a better way, we can further condition you to utilize more empowering thought patterns to the point where they become your default way of thinking, which will help you to produce the most outstanding results possible.

This is my message, but it's not for everyone. It is only for those willing to listen.

UNDERSTANDING THE GROWTH MINDSET

"it's not always the people who start out the smartest who end up the smartest."
—Carol S. Dweck

Having a growth mindset means you are a lifelong learner that explores yourself and the wide-ranging spectrum of fantastic resources the world has to offer to create your own reality while simultaneously inspiring others to do the same. You believe that your talents, abilities, and intelligence can be developed through learning and effort. The opposite of a growth mindset would be described as a limited or fixed mindset.

I expanded upon the growth mindset in the 50 bullet points below, the vast majority of which we will discuss throughout this book. It's a long list, but when I put it together, I had a tough time leaving things out. I could have easily put 100 or more, but for the sake of simplicity, I kept it to 50. In any case, I encourage you to highlight the principles that most intrigue you.

1. Work harder on yourself than anything else.

2. Give so much time to the improvement of yourself that there is no time to criticize others.

3. Miss a meal, but don't miss your reading.

4. We must do one of two things: feed the mind or fall behind.

5. Think, work for, and expect the best.

6. Always make sure your actions align with your affirmations.

7. Look at the bright side of everything and make your optimism come true.

8. Be just as enthusiastic about the success of others as you are about your own.

9. Be a serious student of life.

10. Don't just get through the day, get from the day – join the university of life.

11. Building a lifestyle is cumulative; everything you do matters and moves you closer to your goals.

12. Learn all you can so you can become all you were created to be.

13. Never sacrifice yourself for others. "I'll do for you if you do for me" is selfish. Instead, say "I'll take care of me for you if you take care of you for me." **ADD** value to relationships, don't subtract.

14. Never go with the flow; direct the flow.

15. Live by design.

16. Live with intention.

17. Anyone can do anything in this world.

18. Take control of your health, your relationships, and ultimately your destiny.

19. Commit to continual growth and development.

20. Learning is your superpower.

21. The more you know, the less you need to say.

22. Create a life you don't need a vacation from.

23. Set goals for what they will make of you to achieve them.

24. Learn as a student, not as a follower.

25. You must either minimize your goals or magnify your skills.

26. There is no failure, only results.

27. Be a giver, not a taker.

28. Don't be the person who says, "thank God it's Friday", because those are the people that get to the end of life and say, "thank God it's over."

29. Surround yourself not with people who have what you want, but with people who believe what you believe.

30. Your philosophy is the most significant deciding factor in how your life turns out.

31. Don't hope for a change; make the change.

32. Let discipline be the bridge between your goals to your accomplishments.

33. Don't play it safe by flying low. You may feel comfortable, but you'll never grow.

34. Fly closer to the sun. (see #33)

35. Take responsibility, give away credit.

36. Trust the process of life.

37. Dream big but start small, then connect the dots.

38. Invest in yourself.

39. Respect yourself.

40. Start viewing *setbacks* as *setups* and *trouble* as *transportation.*

41. Let gratitude serve as the golden frame to the picture of a life you have designed for yourself.

42. Have the ability to hold your ego lightly.

43. Build confidence by following through on the promises you make to yourself.

44. If you want to walk on water, you've got to be willing to get out of the boat, to step into the unknown.

45. Learning, practicing, skill-building, and growing increase confidence and diminish fear.

46. If you don't know something, you can surely learn it; if you don't have a specific skill, you can surely build it.

47. Explore possibility.

48. Create reality.

49. Inspire others to explore the possibilities and create reality.

50. Learn all you can and takes notes but always make sure your actions are the product of your own conclusion.

You might be thinking, "Well, Jordan, this all sounds well and good, but what does it all mean for me and my life?"

Indeed, it is all well and good. Throughout our journey together, we're going to develop a deeper conceptual understanding of the growth mindset principles and you will figure out how to apply them to your life.

At this point, it's entirely possible that you may feel a bit skeptical about the importance of a growth mindset. Let's address that before we dive any deeper.

THE SCIENCE OF GROWTH

Philosophers have long theorized self-improvement as a means of achieving well-being, and a lack thereof as a sure path to misery.

Plato believed "If a man neglects education, he walks lame to the end of his life."

Aristotle said things such as, "The educated differ from the uneducated as much as the living from the dead," and "Education is an ornament in prosperity and a refuge in adversity."

More recently, we've uncovered some fascinating

psychological science. A JOHS (Journal of Happiness Studies) study[1] that includes 132 references indicates that personal growth is conducive to feeling the need to contribute to future generations and guide others while simultaneously leading to wisdom and happiness. People with a growth mindset are intelligent, happy givers.

Another study[2] indicates that merely being in a state of readiness and openness to self-improvement (having a growth mindset) leads to greater well-being and life satisfaction.

In a study involving 96 depressed adults, reading caused significant changes in depressive symptoms and thought patterns, which were maintained at follow-up.[3] This explains part of my experience.

Only limited research exists on the reading of self-help growth-oriented books in correlation to diminishing depression and increasing happiness, a sad omission. However, of the research I did find, there is evidence to suggest reading these types of books is helpful.[4, 5] I can tell you quite confidently that reading these books makes a big difference in my life and I know it does the same for my most happy and successful peers.

Tom Corley, author of *Rich Habits: The Daily Success Habits of Wealthy Individuals*, has done extensive research into correlations between reading and success. In terms of income, 85 percent of rich people (in this research, rich is defined as $160,000 yearly or a net worth of $3.2 million) read two self-improvement or educational books *per month*, while only 15 percent of poor people (defined as less than $35,000 yearly or a net worth of under $5k) read those same types of books.[6]

Reading has also been found to decrease stress levels, lower the risk of Alzheimer's disease, and stave off memory decline due to aging.[7]

A 2016 study found that a growth mindset reliably predicts

achievement.[8] The researchers examined the relationship between mindset and intelligence, specifically a growth mindset's impact on students' test scores. In the study, it had been established that the lower a family's income, the lower a student's test score would be. This was because students from these low-income families were more likely to have a fixed mindset than students from higher-income families. After reviewing the scores, they found that students in the lowest tenth percentile of family income received test scores as high as students from the highest income families (80th income percentile). These results showed that mindset could nullify the effects of economic disadvantage regarding intelligence.

Fascinating.

CONFIDENCE ARISING FROM GROWTH

Whenever we lack confidence in any area of our lives, it's usually because we haven't put in the prerequisite work and effort that builds confidence. Perhaps when we are not confident in our ability to give a speech, it is because we have not prepared adequately to give a speech. After all, Benjamin Franklin said, "By failing to prepare, you are preparing to fail." I find this to be true in my life, and the lives of the most successful people in the world.

Nobody was born with confidence. Instead, confident people put in the hard work, effort, preparation, practice, and personal development to increase their confidence. Surgeons were not confident in their ability to repair human beings until they learned how to do so in medical school. Speakers are not confident in their speeches until they practice over and over. Nobody is born with confidence in anything, *ever*.

I was never confident in my ability to be successful until I did the extra reading, sought out mentors, and sought out various other resources. Now, I have a conviction that I will be successful. I have the utmost confidence that I will be who I want to be and do what I want to do. And slowly but surely, I am beginning to realize my vision of success due to the hard work, effort, dedication, preparation, practice, personal development, and the trials and errors I have put myself through over the past few years. Everything is falling into place because I am confident in my abilities to make things fall into place. I am not lucky, and I was never born confident. In fact, I believe *anyone* can be confident in and perform in any arena of life with a bit of practice in that arena.

I can boil my findings down to one phrase: **To increase confidence, increase competence.** When we grow, learn, skill-build, and improve in *anything* we want to do in life, our confidence inevitably increases. And because repetition is the mother of skill, the more we practice something, the better our ability, which increases our confidence even further. **We can master any skill we want in life. All we must do is** *decide* **to do so.**

My friends, this is the most powerful part of having a growth mindset, because **growth leads to confidence, and when we are confident, levels of fear decrease and we can tackle any challenge that comes our way.**

SEEDS OF GREATNESS

"Act is the blossom of thought; and joy and suffering are its fruits; thus does a man garner in the sweet and bitter fruitage of his own husbandry"
—James Allen, As a Man Thinketh

News Flash: there are no seeds of greatness that have been placed inside of us. This is something that needs to be understood by the world because people walk around thinking they are just inherently great without putting in any real effort to be great. They just think they *are* great. This is BS. These people are what we refer to as *entitled*.

The good news is that we can plant seeds of greatness within us whenever we please. Our minds are gardens and the choice of what to feed it with, seeds of greatness or seeds of weeds, is entirely up to us.

PRINCIPLE 1:

Adopt a growth mindset and drop limiting beliefs.

Chapter Resources: Welcome message, Growth Mindset TED Talk by Carol Dweck.

JordanParisHealth.com/gmu-backpack

CHAPTER 2

FEED THE MIND
OR FALL BEHIND

"Education is the passport to the future, for tomorrow belongs to those who prepare for it today."
—Malcolm X

GROWTH

MINDSET

UNIVERSITY

"I want to have a big library room in my house one day so that when people walk in, I can say, 'this is my knowledge.'"

Brett, a 15-year-old client of mine, tells me this as we stretch out on our yoga mats before a session. He then goes on to tell me that he's read three books in the past week.

"You must be a fast reader.", I say.

"Nope, I'm very slow, I just read 4 hours a day.", Brett says back.

Note to self: No more excuses for being a slow reader!

On top of all that, he then goes on to teach me about key philosophies from one of the recent books he's read, *Rich Dad, Poor Dad*, and how these have changed the way he lives.

I stood there dazzled by three things.

1. His dedication

2. His intelligence and awareness

3. He's 15!

When we had started training seven months prior, I never would have imagined him to have such a passion for learning and living.

Fast forwarding six months, Brett and I have been training together for over one year at the time of this writing and he is one of my most cherished friends. He's kept on reading, has developed unbelievable public speaking skills, and has become a fantastic actor and ranks highly in competitions as a result of continually working his craft, which increases his confidence. He's done this all while working five days per week *and* going to school eight hours per day, but he never lets those things get in the way of becoming his best self.

It's rare to see such strong character in a person this young and I've never been so proud and excited for someone before.

At this rate, Brett is well on his way to a successful life on the fulfilling path. He is leaps and bounds ahead of every other kid his age I've ever seen.

THE FALLING BEHIND

"If you feed your mind as often as you feed your stomach, then you'll never have to worry about feeding your stomach or a roof over your head or clothes on your back."
—Albert Einstein

You may have noticed a key phrase at the beginning of the last paragraph; I said, "at this rate." Rates are cool. If you like numbers and sports statistics as I do, rates can be very fun to calculate and look at. If you're an entrepreneur, you can soar to dizzying heights if you calculate what you make on a good day and multiply it by the number of days in a year to see the income you're *on pace* to bring in.

However, even if you're not an entrepreneur, you and I both know that rates aren't always accurate. But if one is naïve enough to believe that one good day indicates that the next 364 will be just as good, then all is well and good for that one day, until the next day when performance is not quite as good. This person soon comes crashing down and the pain felt is proportional to the dizzying heights they had reached just a day before.

We can say the same for going to the gym. When you work out, you might be *on pace* to be fit for life, but we know you cannot go to the gym once and be fit for life.

So, you go to the gym three days in a row.

"Am I fit for life yet?"

No.

So, you go to the gym five days per week for the next six weeks.

"Am I fit for life now?"

Again, you and I can figure this one out quite easily. The answer is a resounding "no" from anyone who's current place of residence is not located under a rock. It's common sense, right?

But let's pretend you reside under that rock. A few days down the line, you're wondering why you don't have abs. Then a year later you're wondering why you're overweight. Now you're falling behind while everyone else is working their asses off at the gym five days per week, 30 minutes daily until the end of time. They're fit now and they will be for life because they're committed to constant growth. In 20 years, you are deeply saddened and confused when your doctor tells you that you're at an elevated risk for heart attack or stroke.

The committed are enjoying the fruits of their labor while the naïve have fallen behind, almost permanently, in health.

Here's another fun example: you say to your significant other, "I love you." You do it one time. Maybe it was on Valentine's day or their birthday. Fantastic. But does that mean you're off the hook for telling them you love them for the rest of eternity?

No way! If only it were that easy (I'm kidding ... I think)!

But then again, maybe you live under that rock. You tell them you love them that one time. Great. Then you don't plan on saying it ever again. You think you're in the clear. You don't know any better. No pain, not yet at least. Life is good.

Then after one week, you wonder why they're upset at you. By week four, they tell you they feel underappreciated and that you aren't making them feel good.

Perplexed, you reply, "What? Why? I said I love you."

Your significant other thinks you're an idiot.

After a few more weeks (or months if they fear the uncertainty of finding someone else), your significant other might leave you for not expressing your love and gratefulness to have them in your life. You are deeply saddened and confused.

Now someone else falls in love with your significant other. They get married. You've been forgotten and left in the dust. It is a sad time. You've fallen behind.

What if you went to college for one day?

You go into a job interview and you go, "Hey hey now, I went to school, so I'm educated."

The employer sees that you do not have a degree and asks you to elaborate. You say you went to college that one day. Someone else got the degree and did the extra reading and skill-building. Someone else gets the job. You're jobless. You're broke. You've fallen behind. It's because you didn't stick with it and do the extra reading and skill-building.

There are many scenarios just like these, where if people do not commit to constant growth and development, they will end up falling behind, forgotten, and in a world of hurt.

So, why do we go to school for however many years, merely fulfilling the education baseline, and then feel as if we never need to learn anything new again?

"I went to school. I did my time. I went through years of training to be able to do what I do."

Sure, you may have gone to school for a long time and completed a good amount of training, but that does not mean you never need to learn and actively skill-build again, unless you wish to peak right here right now.

And what if your job is in a dying or dead industry, like a sewing machine operator? Or a switchboard operator? Or a mail sorter? Or a milkman? Ice cutter? Assembly line worker? And what about the town crier?

Would people with these jobs ever have to go through some more training and education?

If they want to make a living and not fall behind on their bills at the very least, then the answer is yes, *of course.* It's another one of those common sense questions.

What if the field you were in or the job you trained for was no longer needed in ten or twenty years? With all the innovation and automation that has been created in the past twenty years, you never know. Nowadays, when I invest my money, I use a free trading platform like Robinhood to buy whatever I want, or even better; I use an app like Acorns to automatically create a diverse portfolio that suits my risk tolerance and financial goals. Each week, I have an automatic deposit that goes into Acorns, which distributes my investment among various index funds, stocks, and bonds that minimize my risk and maximize my return. My point here is that the middle man is essentially gone. Screw a broker; I have my automated online platforms that save me time and money. Could something like this happen to your industry at some point?

Now let's look at the idea of falling behind on an even larger scale. We started on a micro level, with being fit and relationships. Then we increased the scale when we looked at entire industries. Now we're going to examine the impact of failure to improve or evolve on a macro level.

Think of all the species that have become extinct. Most have been eliminated from the face of the earth due to failure to adapt to certain factors such as climate change, the changing chemical make-up of the environment, inbreeding, mutations, disease, habitat destruction due to humans or other factors, and more dominant predators (humans and more).

Certain species simply failed to adapt and, consequently, were wiped off the face of the Earth. Not to be harsh, but that's what happened. They fell behind.

Those are significant consequences if you ask me.

If you're reading this book, it means you're a human; you are part of a species that has not failed to adapt *yet*.

The warrah, a type of wolf found exclusively on the Falkland Islands, never learned to fear the humans that hunted them. They became extinct. They fell behind.

The same thing happened to the dodo bird. They just didn't learn more than what they already knew and they ended up suffering the consequence of ceasing the ability to exist.

Alright, by now you probably think I'm just trying to scare you into learning, but that's not it. I promise you won't fall off the face of the Earth if you don't read, learn, and skill-build!

However, I can say with confidence that there will be some consequences one way or another. If you're not reading, learning, and actively developing new skills (a.k.a. feeding your mind), someone else is. And that person is going to get the job over you, every time. That person is going to be noticeably better than you in most areas of life, including the most crucial areas, and those are joy and fulfillment.

Living to learn is an unbelievably essential prerequisite to fulfillment. When we stop learning, when we stop growing, when we stop chasing goals, when we become fixed in our skills and our mindsets, then we begin to die. Desire wanes, joy is fleeting, life is dull, and the fire goes out.

At the end of learning, there is nothing left.

I mentioned this very briefly earlier, but I feel the need to emphasize this: **No matter how old you are and no matter how** much success you have achieved, if you stop learning, then you are not living your best life because you've capped the height to which you can rise. You have peaked.

If you've already achieved success and mild fulfillment without personal development, then get ready to take your life to the next level.

Unquestioned Intent

One of the things I've learned through my experiences in communication is that you should never ever question someone's intent.

Think about it logically: When someone accuses you of not caring or not trying, you might feel offended or annoyed. Depending upon the situation, you may even experience anger. I know I've been there.

When I was a college cheerleader, situations like this came up just about every day. If I wasn't perfect, if I didn't throw this girl in the air, catch her feet in my hands with flawless coordination, then extend her over my head and balance her on one foot in a sort of statue of liberty pose, then as soon as it would come down I would hear, "Ugh, I feel like you're not trying." My intent was questioned. Disgustingly offended, I would go into shutdown mode. Then I really didn't want to try any harder, as if it were possible in the first place. This is why I left.

Why do I tell you this story?

I tell you because I want to make it entirely clear that I'm not trying to question you're intent. I know you're trying you're very hardest to live your best life and to live fulfilled, and I want to help you do that if you haven't done it yet. All I'm saying is that there's more for you to *explore*. I found a more fulfilling path and I'm showing it to you so that you may have the opportunity to travel it with me if you so choose to do so. It's entirely your choice though. I'm just opening the door.

MINIMIZE YOUR GOALS OR MAGNIFY YOUR SKILLS

We've already established that simply hoping for things to fall into place doesn't always work. This is especially true when it comes to goals. We cannot hope to give a TED Talk without working on our public speaking skills. We cannot hope to become a professional athlete without putting in thousands of hours of training over many years. We cannot hope to become high-ranking executives without mastering the job we already have, going the extra mile on that job, and doing some additional skill-building on our own. We cannot hope to become millionaires without putting in the work it takes to get there and we definitely won't be able to buy that beach house. Some people go so far as to slack off when they don't hold the executive position they want, give up because they haven't gone pro yet, and never try practicing speech because they haven't been given an opportunity yet. The worst part is that not having what they want is how they justify not putting in the extra effort. These people will stay where they are forever because of this fundamental flaw in their thinking. Do not let this be you.

Here's the key, and it involves a decision: We must either minimize our goals or magnify our skills.

The successful completion of any goal comes from someone *deciding* to magnify their skills. The most successful people don't accomplish their goals out of sheer luck; it is no coincidence that they become so successful. First, they made a congruent and committed decision to do whatever it is they wanted to do. Then they put in the hard work, time, and effort that it was going to take to reach that goal.

Need vs. Want

We don't always get what we *want*. In the same way, we don't always do the things we *should* do. Rather, we get the things we *must have* and we do the things we *must do*. When asked how they did it, the most successful people in the world admit "they had to do it."

On a macro level, people do remarkable things when their level of necessity is high.

On a micro level, many people wait until the last minute to get things done because this is when necessity is the highest. By the way, this is called procrastination, and it stems from a low level of necessity in combination with a goal that doesn't have a whole lot of meaning to you. **There are no procrastinators (in terms of identity) in this world, just low necessity and meaningless goals that make us feel** *busy* **rather than** *productive.*

The question becomes: How can I elevate my level of necessity so that things I *want* **to do become things I** *must* **do?**

BUILDING A LIFESTYLE IS CUMULATIVE

"Success is nothing more than a few simple disciplines, practiced every day."
—Jim Rohn

Everything we do 100 percent of the time counts. It's not about the things we do *some of the time*, or much less, the things we . do once. It's the consistent actions that count and move us closer to our goals.

I'm doing well for myself *so far* at the age of 20. *At this rate*, I'll do all sorts of wonderful things, I'll be the proud owner of equities of all kind. In fact, I already am.

But if the work I do every single day came to a screeching

halt tomorrow, then I wouldn't do much of anything for myself, for the world, and I wouldn't even come close to becoming all I was created to be. I would fall behind. I would be a complete failure if I stopped tomorrow.

If my client, Brett, stopped learning and mastering skills tomorrow, he too would fall behind. He might even fail, but he is aware of this pitfall.

If a professional athlete stopped training tomorrow, his or her performance would almost certainly decline. The athlete would fall behind and out of the league.

If us humans stopped adapting to the everchanging universe, we would surely die off eventually.

If we stopped earning money tomorrow, we would go broke.

The principle is the same with growth; If we stopped learning new things and developing new skills tomorrow, we would become unbelievably bored and any momentum toward a goal we had going would come to a screeching halt.

PRINCIPLE 2:

Feed the mind or fall behind.

Chapter Resources: Proof of evolution on your body video. JordanParisHealth.com/gmu-backpack

CHAPTER 3

DEVELOP YOUR

UNIQUE INSPIRATION

"Where there is no vision, the people perish: but he that keepeth the law, happy is he."
—Proverbs 29:18

GROWTH

MINDSET

UNIVERSITY

Why do you get out of bed in the morning?

Are you excited to get out of bed in the morning? Or do you just get up because you have to?

A major key to excitement, joy, love of life, and fulfillment is the creation of an empowering vision of the world and your place in it.

When we know why we do what we do, not only are we inspired but so are the people around us. A human with a vision sticks out like a sore thumb; we know why they do what they do and what they do only proves it. Even their values are evidently apparent through their vision.

Our vision is what makes us feel alive. It's the internal fire that burns inside of us. It is a fire that should not be lit by anyone but ourselves.

Inspiration vs. Motivation

"Motivation is a fire from within. If someone else tries to light that fire under you, chances are it will burn very briefly."
—Stephen Covey

The quote above by Stephen Covey is fantastic, but I think he may have meant to say "inspiration" instead of "motivation." I actually dislike the word "motivation." I think people often misuse it when they mean to say inspiration. Allow me to expand on this idea.

Motivation is external. Motivation is fleeting; it comes and goes. Motivation *pushes* people to do things. Doing what motivates us doesn't always leave us fulfilled at the end of the day.

Inspiration is internal. It's a feeling deep down inside someone. Inspiration is sustainable. Inspiration acts like a gravitational *pull* that moves us closer to our goals. Doing what inspires us leaves us fulfilled.

Look at it this way: People are often *motivated* by money. Nobody says they're *inspired* by money. That wouldn't make sense. Money doesn't inspire people with a deep-down feeling and it doesn't give someone a sense of fulfillment. Money is just an external motivator for people.

So, we must stop and think: Is what I'm after motivating me or inspiring me?

Happy New Year!

Have you ever wondered why New Year resolutions almost always fail?

It all boils down to external motivation vs. internal inspiration.

A New Year resolution is an external motivator. We attach a meaning to the new year like, "Oh, I'm going to get a six-pack, I'm going to eat healthily, and I'm going to end this toxic relationship." People are saying, "Happy New Year" and the air is filled with hope and excitement.

However, the motivation to achieve your New Year resolution is probably only going to last as long as the celebration that night. What does that resolution mean on January 13th? What's it going to mean on February 13th? All of a sudden, it's March 13th and you're sitting at a burger joint chowing down, no six-pack, no healthy eating, sitting across from the toxic person. You forgot all about what you were trying to do because the external motivator (the new year) is gone and the fire went right along with it. Nobody is walking around on March 13th saying, "Happy New Year!"

The external motivation of the New Year pushes us; never *push* through anything. Rather, find deep inside yourself the internal inspiration, the vision to *pull* you toward the successful completion of your goals. Visualize yourself achieving your goals. Think about how you would feel accomplishing these goals, all the emotions. Imagine what achieving it might make of your character. Imagine how every aspect of your life would be different at the successful completion of these goals and you will find the internal inspiration to *pull* you through very quickly. Do this, and soon you'll want it bad enough that you cut yourself off from any other option. Your level of necessity will be through the roof! And don't just do this at the start of a New Year; do it any day of the year. Do it any day you want to feel more alive, more excited, more joyful, and more fulfilled. Anytime you want something, figure out what it's going to take to get it, develop a plan, and visualize the successful completion of that goal, feel it. Go even further in elevating necessity by realizing the emotions behind the reason you want to change. For example, if you're obese and want to lose 50 pounds, then what's going to happen if you don't change your lifestyle? Well, put simply, you might die a lot sooner than you expect and you might not get to live for certain things you've been waiting for, like your children's graduation.

Confidence Arising from Clarity

Believe it or not, knowing our vision, our inspiration, our very reason for being helps us to build self-confidence (different from cockiness. To learn more about this distinction, visit JordanParisHealth.com/gmu-backpack). Knowing that internal inspiration *pulls* us toward our goals much like gravity, we are more likely to follow through on the promises we make to ourselves, which are our goals (big and small).

Confidence is another one of those things that should be an inside job. We build a sustainable source of confidence internally by following through on the promises we make to ourselves. When we do what we say we're going to do, it feels good. Then we're more likely to make more promises to ourselves, accomplishing more goals and returning greater value to the world as a product of our own outstanding results.

Having this sort of confidence makes you a world-beater because nothing can stop you from doing what you set out to do. In the presence of confidence, fear is not to be found.

GENERATE PROSPERITIES OF ALL KIND WITH CLARITY

Some people walk through life bored because they don't have a purpose, cause, or belief that *pulls* them out of bed in the morning, and that saddens me because nobody should live like that. This is called **aimlessness; it's a vice.**

Very recently, I was volunteering in my town. I was working with two other guys that were my age. While we were taking a break, I was sitting in this chair just looking up at the ceiling with one of those peacefully happy grins on my face as I thought about my diverse portfolio of short, mid, and long-term goals. All of these goals, *what* I want to do, support my vision.

With a clear vision and a portfolio of goals and passion projects that align with my vision, I effortlessly live each day with excitement, joy, love of life, fulfillment, and prosperities of all kind. **The equation is quite simple; clarity of vision in, prosperities out.**

Now let's come back to the scene I described while

volunteering. After I sat there grinning and pondering life for a few minutes, I look to the other guys and say, "Do you ever just get really excited about life?"

One of them, who was there as a requirement after being arrested for drug possession, looked at me confused, let out an all-knowing chuckle and proceeded to say in the most monotonous expression of boredom I have ever heard in my life, "I just want to be able to smoke again."

I like this kid, and I know many others that like him too. In fact, we're friends. But this is not a fruitful way to live. His lifestyle can be expressed by another straightforward equation, which just so happens to be the reverse of the equation I mentioned above: **no vision, no excitement.** Unfortunately, too many people seem to be stuck in the matrix of this disempowering equation.

What about the other guy? Well, he didn't say anything at the time I asked the question, but he did strike up a conversation with me a few hours later in private to tell me about his vision. He was excited to get to work on it, and I was genuinely excited for him too because he has something good to live for.

These are two different kinds of people living by two strikingly different equations. One equation produces an explosively fulfilling life of growth and giving while the other produces nothing. Maybe the latter produces monotony and despair, but I would say that's equal to "zero," a low quality of life. Nothing.

No vision, no excitement.

Clarity of vision in, excitement and other prosperities out.

TO BE DEVELOPED

"In life, people tend to wait for good things to come to them. And by waiting, they miss out. Usually, what you wish for doesn't fall in your lap; it falls somewhere nearby, and you have to recognize it, stand up, and put in the time and work it takes to get to it. This isn't because the universe is cruel. It's because the universe is smart. It has its own cat-string theory and knows we don't appreciate things that fall into our laps."
—Neil Strauss

Often, I hear nonsense like, "I haven't found what I'm passionate about yet," as if the thing that sets their soul on fire is going to appear in front of them one day on a silver platter. Unfortunately, this is not how the world works. **Inspiration, values, and purpose are not** *found.* **Rather, they must be** *developed,* **and the only way to develop these necessities of life is by actively exploring; exploring varieties of books, learning new concepts, building new skills, putting yourself in new situations, and challenging your current assumptions.**

FIRST KNOW, THEN CREATE

"Aimlessness is a vice, and such drifting must not continue for him who would steer clear of catastrophe and destruction."
—James Allen

You can't hit a target you can't see.

In the same way, without having a clear purpose for our lives, we cannot become all we were created to be.

People wander around aimlessly just doing whatever feels good at the moment without considering the long-term ramifications of their actions. They don't have a vision and they don't know what their purpose is for being, so everything is just a blur. They don't care about anything. They're deeply confused by the meaning of life. With a lack of vision and purpose, they never know which opportunities to say yes to and which opportunities to say no to. They are in a constant state of flux, and they end up destroying their lives and only realizing when it is too late. They've gone with the flow so long that it's too late.

Don't let this be you, dear reader. I know you can merit a higher quality of life, a more exciting life, a life of purpose, a life of prosperity. This requires some exploring, which we will get into next chapter.

We may not know the exact purpose of our lives in this very moment, but we can articulate one now and tweak it as we grow, learn, and morph into our best selves. We don't need an end all be all purpose written down on paper within the next five minutes, but we certainly need something articulated if we hope to direct our lives rather than be ordained by circumstance.

It is time to set our sails in the direction we wish to go.

"It is the set of the sails, not the direction of the wind that determines which way we will go."
–Jim Rohn

PRINCIPLE 3:

Develop your purpose.

Chapter Resources: Cocky vs. confident: a personal account of my struggle, Clarity is power video with Tony Robbins.

JordanParisHealth.com/gmu-backpack

CHAPTER 4

INVEST IN YOURSELF

"The more that you read, the more things you will know. The more that you learn, the more places you'll go."
—Dr. Seuss

GROWTH

MINDSET

UNIVERSITY

Invest in yourself – the classic tweet that thousands end up retweeting when a public figure posts it, even though most have no sense of how to invest in themselves. It just sounds good, so it gets retweeted. That's fine, at least it's something positive to spread across the internet.

But what does this statement mean?

To me, it means to work harder on yourself than anything else, and to follow through on doing so.

I guess that begs the question, "What can you do to work hard on yourself?"

Excellent question. This chapter is filled with habits, suggestions, and resources that you can begin to implement into your life today so that you can grow into your best self. This is where you will learn how to invest time and energy into developing the skills you need to advance your vision of the world, your best self's place in it, and find joy in each day.

I don't know about you, but I have this image of myself at my highest potential stuck in my head. I'm not that man yet, but when I get to the end of life, I want to be able to look him in the eye and truly know that man. I don't want him to be a stranger. I want to know him and what it felt like to be him. In fact, I want to *be* him. And by learning and developing new skills, I'm becoming more of that man with each passing day.

Major Key Alert

Continual growth and development is the key to happiness.

Continual growth and development is the key to health.

Continual growth and development is the key to wealth.

Continual growth and development is the key to fulfillment.

Continual growth and development is the key to prosperities of all kind.

A prosperous life is yours for the taking if you can master the art of investing in yourself every single day.

That's the whole key to a prosperous life: Find a few simple ways to invest in yourself that make sense for you and do it *every single day.*

I'd like to emphasize *every single day*, as we discussed that it's not about the things you do only *some* of the time, but instead it's about the things you do *consistently* because building a lifestyle is cumulative. Remember when we discussed how you couldn't just go to the gym one time and be fit for life? You must go to the gym consistently. Well, growth works similarly. It accumulates and accumulates and accumulates, eventually turning into a life of prosperity. I can't tell you the exact day that your life is going to become prosperous, but I can assure you that it will happen eventually. It's a process. Trust it. It's the same with going to the gym; I can't tell you the exact day you will get into shape, but I can assure you that you will get into shape if you go to the gym every single day. We've proven that scientifically. I call this the Law of Accumulated Prosperity, which states the following:

<u>Jordan's Law of Accumulated Prosperity</u>

The result of consistently investing in one's self is a prosperous life, and it's those consistent acts that matter more than any one act of intensity.

It's a pretty simple law. You might even say that it's common sense, and I wouldn't disagree with you. But so many people don't implement this law into their lives. They think they're golden and that they know it all. They think it's endgame (there's no such thing as endgame), the same way I thought I was set for life with the knowledge I already had. I thought I was right. **We all think we are right**, which brings us to the next law.

Jordan's Law of Accuracy
We are all wrong.

Remember when people thought cigarettes were not unhealthy? Remember when we thought Santa was real? Remember when we thought the world was going to end all those times? Those assumptions were all wrong, at least I think the last one was wrong (you and I are still here).

"There are no facts, only interpretations."
—Friedrich Nietzsche

Ordinary people and scientists alike have been predicting different dates that the world will end for thousands of years. All have been wrong so far. There are plenty more predictions in the years to come that all claim such precise things will happen, which make them seem so unlikely. For example, there are multiple claims that asteroids between three and ten kilometers wide will impact Earth and wipe everything out in the next billion years. Then there are supposedly gamma-ray bursts that will occur 300,000 years from now and 550 million years from now. Then there is apparently a supervolcanic eruption that will happen one million years from now. It is also speculated that dramatic drops in carbon dioxide levels of our atmosphere will make Earth uninhabitable in 500 million years and, if not at that time, then again in 1.3 billion years. Between one and five billion years from now, the sun is supposed to end its current phase of development and become 632 times larger than it is right now, which will either consume Earth or at least scorch it. In 3.3 billion years, there is a claim that Jupiter's gravity could make Mercury collide with Venus, which could also lead to a collision into Earth. The entire universe is supposed to end in 22 billion years, but only if a model of dark energy where w = 15 proves to be true (whatever that means, I don't know what "w" is either). In 10 duotrigintillion (a "1" followed by 100 zeros, or simply "googol") years from now, there is a scientific theory that the universe diminishes to a state of no thermodynamic free energy (again, whatever that means), in which case the entire world will no longer sustain motion or life.

I'm no scientist, but most of that is probably wrong in one way or another simply because humans were the ones that figured this stuff out with human-engineered technology, but I guess that makes me wrong for stating these claims are wrong (oh boy, I've taken this too far). But hey, even if some of this stuff happens, there is no way some human figured it out so precisely as to determine the exact year or size of an asteroid or whatever. I just refuse to believe it. In one way or another, it will be wrong. Every theory of the world ending has been wrong so far and they will likely continue to be.

The Joy of Challenge

There is a considerable joy to be found in being wrong about everything, however, because continually learning, growing, and improving is a fun challenge for us humans. **If we knew it all, life would be boring anyway. Let's embrace the wonders of not** knowing. And let's take it a step further by continually challenging the beliefs and assumptions that we already hold because it would only make sense that doing so would add to the fun. Even better, you'll accumulate a wider variety of perspectives, which will make us wise. This is another critical concept we must understand before we go over how to invest in ourselves.

Jordan's Law of Wisdom
Since we are all wrong and there is an infinite number of things that can be true for any given person (Law of Infinite Truths, to be explained soon), the only path to wisdom is an accumulation of different perspectives.

When we stop to ask ourselves, "How could I be misinterpreting (insert topic here)?", and, "What would it mean if I was wrong?", We open ourselves up to an immense opportunity to expand our minds beyond the level of thinking we currently have. **Remember what Albert Einstein said?** *We can not solve our problems with the same level of thinking that created them.* Similarly, the same level of thinking that got us here will not get us to where we want to go. Therefore, it is necessary to challenge our own assumptions and open ourselves up to new perspectives, which leads to further possibility. There is a great joy to be found in this sort of challenge.

"A bird doesn't sing because it has an answer, it sings because it has a song."
—Maya Angelou

Weathering Storms

Have you ever had a conflict with someone?

I'd be willing to bet that you answered that question with a, "yes", and that's quite alright. It's to be expected if you've ever set foot on this planet, which I assume you have.

In any case, I thought I should mention that the Law of Accuracy is quite useful to keep in mind whenever conflict with others may arise. **In these times of conflict, just assume you are wrong. Assume that the other person knows more than you do. Then say in response to whatever is thrown at you, "I believe what you believe." Saying this will either elicit one of two types of reactions: 1) The person will respond in a less confrontational way than they had previously, or 2) The person will look at you confused for a moment, then they will become even angrier. Responding in this way allows us to differentiate between people who are genuinely upset with us (reaction 1) and people who just want some juicy drama (reaction 2).**

Now, I'll admit that I'm not very good at applying the Law of Accuracy to my conflicts in this manner. I understand that it is quite difficult to hold back once your body goes into fight or flight mode and every fiber of your being wants to stand up for yourself and lash back. This is a simple concept to explain and understand, but it may very well be one of the toughest to apply to our lives. If you can do this, I commend you. If not, it is great to at least keep in mind.

BACK ON TRACK

For a minute there, I lost myself, as we've gone off on a bit of a tangent thus far in this chapter. That's life sometimes though. We get off track. We don't always take the quickest route. Sometimes we make a left turn when we were supposed to go straight, but that's alright. Shit happens. Plus, it always turns out ok in the end, which we'll learn about in chapter six (Trouble is Transportation). It's all good. It's always all good. I easily could have deleted this section to fix it, but I want to be transparent by letting you see the process so that you may learn to trust it. Now, without further ado, we're going to explore the different ways we can turn our handy-dandy *Invest in yourself* tweet into our reality, the reality that we create.

HOW TO INVEST IN YOURSELF (YOUR BEST SELF WILL THANK YOU LATER)

Method #1 – Read Books

In my opinion, this is the best way invest in yourself. But again, I'm usually wrong (why are you still listening to me?!). You may think one of the other methods in this chapter is the best. I'll leave that to you to explore and find out though.

People have taken a lifetime of learning, experience, and truth-seeking and packaged it into books that you can read in a few hours. **You can download a lifetime of knowledge onto your brain in a matter of hours.**

I want to ask you a question before we go any further: If you had to take an open-note test on a particular subject, and you had a whole notebook filled with the answers, wouldn't you want to use that notebook while taking the test? I know I would!

Now imagine that life was an open-note test, and you had the answers in front of you in the form of books (which we all have access to), wouldn't it make sense to use those answers to help guide you? It sure would make sense.

Then how come so many people pass up the opportunity to use the notes available to them during the test even when it is not considered cheating? With smartphones intruding the world, reading seems to have become much less frequent than it used to be. I'm sad to see it. In fact, as part of the most informal study ever conducted on planet Earth, only 27 percent of my Instagram followers reported that they read on a daily basis when I polled them through my story. That means that 73 percent of my peers choose not to use the notes available to them.

This analogy of taking an open-note test portrays how I feel about books in our world, except it's as if I'm cheating because most people don't use these books. But the fact of the matter is that I'm not cheating. **Books aren't illegal yet, are they?**

The knowledge I have gained from the books I've read has proven to be pivotal in the big picture of my journey through life to this point. Although books have never given me exact answers to problems (and they never will), they have effectively pointed me in the right direction of growing into my best self.

What I just said was extremely important; **we cannot be delusional by thinking that books will give us all the answers. Instead, they serve merely as guides that help bring us closer to our best selves by challenging the assumptions and beliefs that we currently hold, which enables us to grow and increase our wisdom due to the accumulation of perspectives. In the same way, this book absolutely will not give you all the precise answers simply because I don't have all the answers myself, and I'm the author of course. We must keep in mind that this is true of all authors; they do not have all the answers, and anyone that says they do is full of crap.**

As we read a variety of different books, we may find that one author says something that completely contradicts what an author of a previous book we read may have said. What gives? Well, it's the Law of Infinite Truths.

<u>Jordan's Law of Infinite Truths</u>

Two opposing statements can be true for different people. For example, what is true for you may not be true for me. Nevertheless, it is true for someone. Therefore, all statements *can* be true.

One statement can be true for you while the opposing statement can simultaneously be true for me. Human beings are not one size fits all. **Everyone has their own unique truths and principles that guide them along the journey of life.** Every pair of contradictory statements can be true for different people, thus resulting in an infinite amount of truths. **You just have to find the truths of your own life through exploring the wide-ranging spectrum of truths from various perspectives and minds through the books that are available to all of us.**

There is a book, and I'm sure you have heard of it, called *Think and Grow Rich*. As Jim Rohn's mentor once said to him, "Think and Grow Rich ... don't you think you ought to read that book?"

Jim read that book and many others, changed his mindset, and proceeded to go from dead broke and in debt to millionaire over the next six years. If you're trying to live a life of prosperity and, well, think and grow rich (which I assume you would like to do), then I would say you ought to read that book too. A book with that title! Imagine what you could learn and apply to your life in the name of thinking and growing rich.

An abundance of books is available for all of us that will help us to learn the principles and develop the skills we must acquire to advance our unique vision of the world, whatever that vision may be. If you want to become a great public speaker, there are scores of books that will teach you everything you need to know to become a great public speaker.

If you want to build a successful business, there are scores of books that will teach you everything you need to know to build a successful business. If you want to learn how to pick up women/men, there are scores of books that will teach you everything you need to know to pick up women/men. If you want to learn how to be the healthiest you can be, there are scores of books that will teach everything you need to know to be the healthiest you can be. If you want to master your thoughts, there are scores of books that will teach you everything you need to know to master your thoughts. If you want to learn how to love and respect yourself, there are scores of books that will teach you everything you need to know to love and respect yourself. If you want to learn how to take action, there are scores of books that will teach you everything you need to know to take action. If you want to learn how to invest money, there are scores of books that will teach you everything you need to know to invest money. If you want to awaken your awareness of the universe, there are scores of books that will teach you everything you need to know to awaken your awareness of the universe. If you want to gain a new perspective, there are scores of books that will give you a new perspective. If you want to learn how to win friends and influence people, there are scores of books that will teach you everything you need to know to win friends and influence people. If you want to learn psychology, there are scores of books that will teach you everything you need to know about psychology. If you want to learn what makes the most successful people in the world different, there are scores of books that will teach you everything you need to know about the most successful people in the world. If you want to change your life, there are scores of books that will teach you everything you need to know to change your life.

The list goes on. My point is that there is undoubtedly a

book for just about everything you could possibly want to learn.

Oh, and in the unlikely event that someone has the excuse that he or she doesn't know how to read and get the most out of a book, there is a book for that too. It's called *How to Read a Book*. It's a classic.

Here are some of my favorite books:

❖ *Awaken the Giant Within* by Tony Robbins
❖ *How to Win Friends and Influence People* by Dale Carnegie
❖ *The Mastery of Love* by Don Miguel Ruiz
❖ *As a Man Thinketh* by James Allen
❖ *Captivate* by Vanessa Van Edwards
❖ *The Sun Does Shine* by Anthony Ray Hinton
❖ *Way of the Peaceful Warrior* by Dan Millman
❖ *Unshakeable* by Tony Robbins
❖ *Ego is the Enemy* by Ryan Holiday
❖ *Man's Search for Meaning* by Viktor Frankl
❖ *Think Better Live Better* by Joel Osteen

These are just a few of the books that helped me along the journey of seeking my own truth and my own principles, the very principles in this book. My complete reading list can be found in this chapter's resources at JordanParisHealth.com/gmu-backpack. It is very easy to read every day because you only need 15 minutes, and if you don't have 15 minutes then you don't have a life. Also, if you are serious about success and fulfillment, then you are going to have to get serious about reading.

"An original idea. That can't be too hard. The library must be full of them."
—Stephen Fry

"The only thing that you absolutely have to know is the location of the library."
—Albert Einstein

Method #2 – Podcasts

Podcasts are audio files that anyone can access for free from their smartphones, and they have revolutionized the way I feed my mind. People produce shows to interview the best and brightest minds in the world and share their insights and principles they've learned over a lifetime with you, and they package it into highly entertaining bite-sized, 40-minute episodes. Here are some of my favorite shows:

- ❖ **Impact Theory** – Impact Theory is hosted by the co-founder of Quest Nutrition, Tom Bilyeu. The stated mission of the podcast is to "end the poverty of poor mindset," which goes along with this book so fantastically. Tom gets inside the minds of some of the most intelligent and impactful human beings on the planet, including Seth Godin, Bob Hariri, Jay Shetty, Mike Posner (he shocked me in his episode), Tim Ferriss, Jim Kwik, Gary Vaynerchuck, Shaun White, Michael Strahan, and many more. The insights I've gained from these incredible people have been priceless in guiding me down the path of fulfillment and success.

- ❖ **The School of Greatness** – The School of Greatness is hosted by the former professional athlete and mega lifestyle entrepreneur Lewis Howes. Lewis has done an excellent job empowering people to take control of their life and business himself (I've even been a student in some of his courses), but he supplements this by interviewing the most exceptional people on the planet. There are over 600 episodes by now, and he pumps out about three per week so we'll never really run out. He brings on guests such as Tony Robbins, Julianne Hough, Grant Cardone, Daymond John, James Altucher, Dr. Mark Hyman, Jack Canfield, Novak Djokovic, Les Brown, Sara Blakely, and many more. The list is freaking outstanding. What's even more outstanding? The lessons these greats teach us; everything from the keys to success, wealth, and fulfillment to memory mastery to the science of people. You'll be left wanting to run through a wall, except you'll be much smarter so you'll find the most efficient way around it.

❖ **Growth Mindset University** – Shameless plug! Growth Mindset University is all about learning the things that we should have learned in school but didn't. Each episode and upgraded guest features a brand new lesson. We're just getting started this and would be delighted if you joined us on this learning journey!

❖ **More Quality Podcasts I Love:** Akimbo with Seth Godin, The Tim Feriss Show, The Tony Robbins Podcast, Bulletproof Radio, Ed Mylett Show, The Jordan Harbinger Show, Joel Osteen Podcast, The Joe Rogan Experience, The Brendon Show, TED Talks Daily, WorkLife with Adam Grant, The Chase Jarvis Live Show, The GaryVee Audio Experience, The Model Health Show.

When I wake up in the morning, I turn on an inspirational or educational podcast that will ground me firmly in the roots of my purpose. All I have to do is hook my phone up to my speaker and I put it on as I prepare for my day. I don't have to budget any time for this. Podcasts help me set a kick-ass tone for the day so that I can feel my absolute best all day and consequently produce the most outstanding results I possibly can.

Car rides have been turned into transformational voyages with the wonders of podcasts. All I have to do is connect my phone to my car, let it play through the speakers, and put on my mental track shoes and run with it. Again, I don't have to budget any time for this because I'll always have to drive. And I still listen to music in the car too (I'm not insane!), I do it roughly one out of every three drives. Listening to music every single moment you're ever in a car gets a little old anyway, so podcasts are an excellent way to switch things up and find balance.

When I'm cooking, I connect my phone to speaker and listen to another excellent podcast as I cook. Yet again, I don't have to budget any time for this because I cook two or three times every day (the healthy thing to do!).

With podcasts, travel days in the airport and flying on planes simply become days at the University of Life, Growth Mindset University. Easy. Simple. Productive. Exciting. Joyous. Those are the words I would use to describe my experience with podcasts.

This stuff is so easy. It's 100 percent free and you never have to budget any time. It's passive, mindless stuff; you just need to cue it up and listen to it (podcasts are great for lazy learners). There are no excuses hear unless you are deaf (pun intended).

I think you'll find that this learning experience becomes addicting, as I have.

Method #3 – Keep an Idea Journal

Invest in a blank journal and you may just be surprised at the equities you can fill it with over time, which will undoubtedly be worth far more than the initial investment you made to purchase the journal. My idea journal is worth millions of dollars at this point, and the best part is that I got it for free. Talk about a winning investment! An idea journal can change your life. It certainly changed mine.

By ideas, I mean ideas for your future, ideas for your business, ideas for your health, ideas for your wealth, ideas for your relationships, ideas for designing your life, ideas about your dreams. **Any idea. Just write it down. Anything that is currently in your head is just a dream. It's not real. You begin making it real the second you put it down on paper. Write it down and your life will explode into change.** Take this journal everywhere with you. Take care of it. Treat it like your baby. **Treasure it, for the buried treasure lies inside.**

"But I don't have good ideas." Just write something down anyway. It could be anything at all. Start writing, and the ideas will come. Don't just wait for ideas to come to you to begin writing. That's what everybody does. They won't come to you on a silver platter. Merely waiting for ideas before starting any work is the same mentality of those who go through life with their fingers crossed, just hoping and praying for a change. This mentality is a cornerstone of the weak, fixed mindset. But that's not you. **You are a creator.** Say it: *I am a creator.* Make it part of your identity. **Simply begin and the rest becomes easier.** This is true of most things in life. For example, **inspiration comes from taking action, not vice versa.** Honestly, I didn't have the entire concept of this book before I started writing. **When I started, all I knew is that I wanted to start. So, I just started writing, then the inspiration came, then the ideas came.** Each night, I have tons of new ideas and concepts for the book running through my mind that never would have risen to the surface had I not performed the act of beginning. **My mind came alive from simply getting started, from taking imperfect** action. Not all action must be perfect. Perfectionists are usually losers because they fail to ever begin.

> *"If you're serious about becoming a wealthy, powerful, sophisticated, healthy, influential, cultured and unique individual, keep a journal ... When you listen to something valuable, write it down. When you come across something important, write it down ... I became a buyer of blank books. People found it interesting that I would buy a blank book. "Twenty-six dollars for a blank book, why would you pay that?" they'd say. Well, the reason I paid it was to challenge myself to find something worth $26 to put in there. But if you ever got a hold of one of my journals, you wouldn't have to look very far to discover that it's worth more than that."*
>
> —Jim Rohn

Method #4 – Good ol' YouTube

YouTube has tremendous content you can use to feed your mind. I'm not referring to the cat videos though. Rather, I'm referring to the abundance of TED Talks, inspirational and educational speeches, seminar clips, interviews, podcasts in video format, skill-building videos, and How To's that are available to all of us for free. Some videos are similar to podcasts in that you can cue something up to play and listen while you do something else like cook, clean, eat, shower, or drive. I've inserted my favorite YouTube videos into this chapter's resource page, as well as what an Impact Theory podcast looks like in video format.

Method #5 – Eat Clean

Sadly, eating clean is often overlooked as a means of investing in yourself, but the reality is that eating clean will give you a ton more energy, which will support you in producing outstanding results in every aspect of your life. To help you begin making the right choices, the diet that I give to my clients is available to you for free in the online resources for this chapter.

Method #6 – Move!

Like eating clean, exercise is another fantastic way to help you look your best, feel your best and obtain more energy, which goes a long way in producing outstanding results in all aspects of your life.

Method #7 – Blog it Out

I started blogging back in December of 2016 just to write about and expand upon the thoughts I had going on in my head. I was a freshman in college, so I was rapidly making new discoveries and forming new ideas about the world at the time. I blogged for my own growth, not necessarily for other people. However, I found that a side effect of my writing was that it also helped and resonated with others, which was a bonus. Additionally, by projecting my thoughts out into the world, I found that it became incredibly easy to walk my talk, live what I preach, and further expand the growth of my mind.

So, here's what I have to say about blogging: 1) I think everybody should start a blog, and 2) I believe that each person's life has some sort of blog-worthy material that the world would benefit from. More bloggers mean a greater diversity of perspectives shared with the world, which is precisely what we need in a world where individuals must seek their own unique truths.

We all have time to blog too, because if you write only 15 minutes per day for 300 days per year, that adds up to a whopping 75 hours over the course of the year, enough time to pump out *hundreds* of posts, which is probably too much.

Method #8 – Be Curious

Be curious about the world. Curiosity brings joy from the wonders of learning. We can be curious about nature; visit a nature trail and notice all the sounds, all the sights. Open your eyes and be present by bringing your attention to the little things around you. Let it all marvel you, let it fascinate you, let it intrigue you. Nature is so beautifully profound.

We can be curious about the universe. With so many billions of galaxies and the billions of years that the universe has (supposedly) existed, there is so much to wonder and learn about. The deeper you dig into trying to find out about the universe, the more your jaw begins to drop as you realize just how much there is still to learn. The universe is so fantastically profound.

We can be curious about human beings. There are over seven billion people on this planet, and each one has unique insights, perspectives, causes, beliefs, and things that make them tick. **I used to hate people, but that's because I was never curious about them.** I thought I had people all figured out, assuming that all of them were the same in that they shared this disempowering characteristic: they all sucked. But that wasn't true. I just needed to get curious. We can learn equally from the best and worst humans on the planet by merely asking questions and sparking conversations that go deeper than surface level. It was the great Galileo that said, "I have never met a man so ignorant that I couldn't learn something from him." Ralph Waldo Emerson added to this empowering statement, saying, "Every man I meet is in some way my superior; and in that, I can learn from him."

Being curious is what makes everything in life beautiful, and there's no stopping curiosity.

"Curiosity is the wick in the candle of learning."
—William Arthur Ward

FIND BALANCE

"Balance. The Ultimate Goal."
—Ricky Lankford

Now, I'm not saying that we should all have our headphones in our ears listening to podcasts half the day and burying your head in books the other half of the day while blocking out the rest of the world. That's not living. I don't advise that. Instead, we must find balance, time to go out and apply what we've learned to the world and see where it takes us. We must also leave time in our day for blank space, a time where we are not engaged in anything at all. No phones, no music, no podcasts, no books, no people. Just ourselves all alone. I find it shocking how few people spend time by themselves. Some people can't even do it at all. They can't even sit by themselves, which is a tell-tale sign that they lack love and respect for themselves. Allow me to explain.

Loneliness and solitude are entirely different. **Loneliness is the poverty of self. Solitude is the richness of self.**

Loneliness is a negative state of isolation. In this state, one can feel lonely even in the presence of others. To be lonely means you lack love and respect for yourself. You rely on the numbing effects of outside influences, much like the way an alcoholic relies on the intoxicating effects of alcohol. **If you cannot enjoy being around yourself, how could you expect others to enjoy being around you?**

Solitude is the state of being alone without feeling lonely. Being able to live in solitude means you have the ultimate love and respect for yourself because you can just enjoy yourself and all life has to offer. You know you don't need anyone or anything else. You are self-sufficient. You are content, and everything else is a bonus.

I lead a productive life, usually surrounded by other people, but I love my alone time, my me time. In fact, I put *Scheduled Me Time* on my schedule daily, and I turn down social outings or other opportunities during that scheduled time block. My alone time is essential for the health of my body, mind, and soul. Scheduled Me Time is non-negotiable. That alone time becomes creation time, inspire time, imagine time, self-realization time; it's where ideas happen. **Often when people say they don't have ideas, it is usually because they don't allow the time for ideas to happen.** Further, mastering solitude is fantastic because you don't need anything or anybody else to make you happy because you can make yourself happy. **Mastering solitude fosters an authentic and sustainable form of happiness.**

TO MASTER THE MIND, BUILD A MASTER CURRICULUM

When building our personal development curriculum, it is essential to not just focus on our strengths, but also our weaknesses. I believe our curriculum should *mainly* focus on our weaknesses and our fears. This is the essence of a multi-dimensional, well-rounded individual.

To become multi-dimensional, well-rounded individuals, we should consider the following questions when determining what we should be learning and the skills we should be developing:

❖ What skills do I need to possess to reach my goals/advance in my career?

❖ What do I really suck at?

The answers to these questions are what our curriculum should focus on.

MASTERY MASTERY MASTERY!

"The truth is that creative activity is one that involves the entire self - our emotions, our levels of energy, our characters, and our minds."
—Robert Greene

Those who dabble are doomed. Those who master move mountains. If we scatter our skills without mastering any particular one, we can expect to feel scatter-brained while only achieving marginal success at best. Learning and skill-building is all about mastery. Once we've identified what we want to learn and what skills we need to build, we need to go all in. Reading a blog post or a Reddit article doesn't result in mastery; reading book after book, seeking mentor after mentor, and taking action after action is precisely what results in mastery. Every single skill I've mastered has been the result of countless books, mentors, and trial and errors. I wasn't born with any unique talent, all I did was commit to mastery. Don't dabble, master.

THE BEST DAY(S) EVER

"You know you're in love when you can't fall asleep because reality is finally better than your dreams."
—Dr. Seuss

You may want to think this is hard to believe, but each day of my life is better than the last. Each day brings a bit more joy than the last. Yesterday was the best day of my life, but today is even better. In the same way, 2016 was the best year of life (that's when I decided to take control of my life). 2017 was even better than 2016. 2018 has already brought twenty-thousand times more joy and fulfillment than 2017 did. And with all the valuable nuggets of knowledge I am learning each day, the new skills I am developing each day, and the new set of goals and passion projects I have planned out that just so happen to align with what I am learning and the skills I am developing each day, 2019 may just be the best year yet. Of course, this all makes sense when we consider the Law of Accumulated Prosperity.

PRINCIPLE 4:

Work harder on yourself than anything else.

Chapter Resources: Reading list, podcasts, Best of YouTube, the LIFE Diet, Health and Fitness Programs, Impact Theory podcast video, being a serious student video with Jim Rohn, how to start your blog.

JordanParisHealth.com/gmu-backpack

PHASE 2

CREATE

"Life isn't about finding yourself. Life is about creating yourself."
—George Bernard Shaw

QUESTIONS FOR ANSWERS

"Successful people ask better questions, and as a result, they get better answers."
—**Tony Robbins**

GROWTH

MINDSET

UNIVERSITY

Discovery is the product of asking questions, but not just any questions. If we want an extraordinary quality of life, we must ask questions that guide us down a path of discovery.

We all have a voice in our heads, and that voice will inevitably ask questions. Whether those questions empower us to be our best selves or whether they disempower us and make us feel like crap is primarily up to us.

My philosophy on questions can be explained with the following statement: better questions result in better answers while poor questions result in poor answers.

Monitoring our self-talk is a challenging skill to master, but it is also a compelling way to create an explosion of change in our lives. The power lies in the fact that our brains, our supercomputers, will come up with an answer to any question we plug into it. Asking ourselves questions is like typing something into a search engine; we are going to get an answer. Whether the answer is empowering or not is obviously dependent upon what we type in. Too often, people let viruses infect their software.

Questions direct our focus, and thus, our quality of life. We cannot expect to live an extraordinary quality of life if the questions we ask are poor. That's not how the equation works. Quality questions in, quality life out. Poor questions in, poor life out.

There are many people on Twitter who put their poor quality of questions, and thus, their reduced quality of life on full display for the world to see. Scrolling through your feed, you'll almost inevitably see things like, "Why does nobody understand?", "Why does this always happen to me?", "What is wrong with our society?", and, "Why do people suck?"

Sad. Even worse is that tons of people eat this stuff up by "liking" it and retweeting it, but when somebody posts something positive, it rarely gets the same level of attention.

As I scroll through my feed right now, I see a tweet with 2,800 retweets and over 11,000 likes that reads, "why is bread bad for u and why does ur tan never look as good as it does in the shower and why is traveling expensive and why is school hard?"

Terrible.

Imagine the plethora of disempowering answers your brain could come up with in response to those questions. How do those questions and answers leave you feeling? Probably terribly disempowered!

If you habitually ask yourself, "why me?" then your brain is going to come up with a disempowering answer. On the contrary, if you ask yourself a better question in a tough situation, like, "what's great about this?" or "what can I learn from this?" then your brain is going to come up with a much more empowering answer.

Let's apply this to the real world. Pretend your significant other has just left you. Naturally, your initial reaction is that of upset and devastation. I'd say that's fair enough, as I've indeed reacted this way many times over. In fact, I usually get more upset than most people when something like this happens, but I never stay in that dark place for too long because of the habitual questions I ask myself. Within 24 hours, I'm feeling incredible!

Now, when you're partner leaves you, you have one of two options: you can ask empowering questions or disempowering questions.

Let's say the first question in your head sounds like, "What is wrong with me?"

By asking this question, you are setting yourself up to answer in a way that sounds like this: "I'm ugly, I'm gross, I'm not good enough, and I pick my nose."

You've already directed your focus to make you feel like crap.

Then you ask, "Why would this person leave me?"

This question sets you up to say, "It's because I'm not good enough, there is someone better than me, and I pick my nose."

Now you feel even worse.

Next, you might type into the search engine, "Why does life suck?"

The search engine will inevitably come up with an answer, perhaps saying, "Life sucks because there are no good people out there and everyone is miserable, and nobody likes me and all good things must come to an end."

After these three questions, which your brain can fire off and receive answers to in a matter of seconds, you are feeling like absolute garbage. The meaning you have attached to the breakup is effectively this: "I suck, life sucks, I'm not good enough."

How incredibly disempowering. The focus of our questions guides the quality of our experiences and the meanings of the events of our lives.

Now let's say you are aware of the fantastic power that questions hold over your life. You know how to direct the questions to empower yourself.

First, you might ask, "What could the deeper meaning be here?"

You think, "Well, maybe that just saved me. Maybe this happened because there is someone much better for me in the future. Maybe this happened because it's time for me to come into a period of post-traumatic growth. Maybe this is for the best."

By asking this question, you've directed your focus to look at the bright side, and you've shaped a higher meaning for what the event means for your life.

But you don't stop there, you ask, "What's great about this?"

"I can use this new chapter of my life to grow, develop myself, and be open to new experiences. I'll have more time to spend with my friends. This could be the most exciting period of my life. I feel free. This is cool."

At this point, you have faith that there is a deeper meaning behind the event. You feel ready to take on the world. You're ready to explore the world and create a new reality for yourself. You've primed yourself to feel excited.

"Well, Jordan, is it really this easy?"

Yes, it is this easy! What else would you do? How else would you shape the meaning and quality of your experiences than by guiding your focus with the power of questions?

Some would say something along the lines of, "Oh, well I'll just be strong."

"Being strong" doesn't work. "Being strong" is putting a mask on to cover up the broken insides. It's like putting the exterior body of a new Porsche on a 50-year-old car that doesn't even run anymore. Don't do that!

I believe that "being strong" is one of the major factors contributing to the fact that men are almost four times as likely to commit suicide than women. Men are told to "be strong," or worse, "be a man." They hide their emotions, and it builds up and up and up until one day it all becomes too much, and that's when the suicide happens.

Don't "be strong" by putting on a mask. Instead, fix yourself from the inside first, then out. It's a holistic way of dealing with challenges. And quite honestly, it's the right way to do it. It's noble. Be a real Porsche, not a fake one.

Let's make a pact. From now on, instead of "being strong" to solve our problems, we will only use empowering questions.

PRIME, PREPARE, PROVIDE (P3)

Not only are questions critical in times of trouble, but they are equally as important in preparing ourselves to produce outstanding results each day. Below is a series of strategic questions I use to set myself up for success each day.

Prime

We can ask questions that prime us to feel a certain way. I call these "priming questions." This type of question can help set our intentions for an activity, an encounter, the day, and even a goal. Being intentional gives us peace of mind and clarity, thus making it less likely that we are distracted or drawn off course while also increasing the likelihood of success astronomically. Below is a list of priming questions you can habitually ask yourself to achieve these outcomes.

- ❖ What can I be excited about today?
- ❖ What can I do to achieve this goal?
- ❖ What am I thankful for?
- ❖ What feelings do I want to experience in my encounter with this person today?
- ❖ What would have to happen to make this a level 10 experience for myself and everyone around me?
- ❖ What were my top three moments today? (then reflect on them, relive them, and be thankful for them)

Prepare

We can ask questions that prepare us for specific situations. I call these "preparatory questions." These questions provide us with a sense of certainty that we will be able to navigate life's toughest challenges. Below is a list of preparatory questions you can habitually ask yourself to be ready to take on any challenge.

> ❖ Who/what might trip me up today and how can I respond?
> ❖ What can I do if _____ happens today?
> ❖ How would my highest self bounce back if _____ does not go as planned?

Provide

We can ask questions that will aid in our search for ways to achieve life's most profound joy, which is genuine fulfillment. These questions help us find ways to find fulfillment and contribute. I call these "providing questions." Below is a list of questions you can habitually ask yourself to achieve this outcome.

> ❖ Who can I surprise with a thank you or a token of appreciation today?
> ❖ Who is someone that would appreciate a short phone call from me today?
> ❖ Who can I give a smile to today? (hint: the answer to this is *everyone*!)
> ❖ What are some things I could bring attention to that help me discover the adventure in a smile?
> ❖ Who needs me to be my best today?
> ❖ Where can I volunteer this week that would align with

my purpose, cause, or belief?

❖ What are some things I could appreciate and meditate on that I usually take for granted? (think about taking that first sip of water, observing nature, the first bite of food, the presence of a good friend)

❖ What did I learn today?

P3

This diverse portfolio of questions collectively makes up what I refer to as the P3. It's my secret weapon for feeling what I want to feel, consistently being my best self, and experiencing real fulfillment.

Triggers

These questions are fantastic at shaping the quality of experiences we have in our lives. But what good is a secret weapon that doesn't have a trigger you can pull?

You guessed it, without triggers, the secret weapon (these questions) becomes useless.

What am I saying?

I mean that we can pretend we're going to use these questions all we want, but unless we have set times or events throughout the day that *prompt* us to use these questions, then we won't use them.

We must have triggers to create habits, which is precisely what we want; we want these questions to become habitual so that you ask them without having to do much thinking.

One of my triggers is the shower. So, each time I shower, which is almost always first thing in the morning, I ask one question from each of the three categories.

Another one of my triggers is this red light outside of my neighborhood that I inevitably get stuck at for a few minutes each time I wish to pay a visit to the wonderful world outside of my sheltered community. Here, I usually ask the question, "What three things can I be grateful for?", which *primes* me to see life through the golden lens that is gratitude.

Perhaps my most important trigger is right before I enter a significant social interaction. I ask myself, "What are the feelings I want to get from this social interaction and what feelings do I want to leave this person with?"

No matter the interaction and specific feeling I want to achieve and leave the other person with, the concept is always this: I want to feel good, and I want to leave the other person feeling uplifted. Imagine how great your interactions would be and how well-liked you would be if you did this with everyone. This interaction trigger is the key to becoming influential.

My last trigger is when I get into bed at night. That is my trigger to ask, "What were my top three moments today?" I *reflect* on the moments, and then I *relive* them. Reliving these moments in your head is quite fascinating because our brains cannot distinguish the difference between real and imagined experiences. So, I get to live my best moments twice every day. This is referred to as *doubling*.

After reflecting and reliving those moments, I apply the golden lens of gratitude. I say, sometimes aloud, "Yeah, that was really cool," or, "I'm glad I got to experience that." Above all else, bring attention to the way you feel as you reflect. **To be peaceful, notice the peace. To be joyful, notice the joy. To be fulfilled, notice the fulfillment. As you notice these wonders, feel the smile that may come across your face; That's the adventure in a smile.**

ADDICTION 101

If you've ever wanted to get rid of the vast majority of the negative self-talk in your head, then this may be your big chance.

You see, we cannot simply get rid of something. Matter is neither created nor destroyed, remember? Instead, we must replace one thing with another, which is why when people who are addicted to cigarettes try to go cold turkey, who stop entirely smoking cigarettes all at once, they usually fail and crawl back to the cigarettes in short order. It's the same with most drugs, alcohol, and even habits. Although possible, it is very challenging to cease from doing something that you have regularly been doing over an extended period without first replacing it with something else.

We can't just get rid of negative thoughts. Instead, we must replace them with more empowering thoughts, which is where our questions come in. We can use our empowering questions as a laser that guides our focus, our thoughts, and our wellbeing.

Replace the bad with the good.

Again, you might say, "Well, Jordan, is it really that easy?"

Yes, it's that easy, where else would you start?

LIFE'S GOLDEN TICKET

Questions are the answers. Remember that. With an extraordinary portfolio of questions, you'll become extraordinary. As we've learned, questions give us the incredible power of guiding our emotions, our creativity, and the order of our entire lives. **If you master the art of questioning, then you master your thought patterns, and you can effectively punch your ticket to the good life, my friend.**

PRINCIPLE 5:

For an extraordinary quality of life, ask an extraordinary quality of questions.

CHAPTER 6

TROUBLE IS
TRANSPORTATION

"Smooth seas do not make skillful sailors. "
—African Proverb

GROWTH

MINDSET

UNIVERSITY

Kyle Maynard is a New York Times bestselling author, moving public speaker, award-winning extreme athlete, and mountaineer that has climbed to the peak of Mount Kilimanjaro. He just so happens not to have any limbs.

I'm telling you about Kyle to show you, and I say this with the utmost respect, that your excuses are probably a bunch of BS. They do not define you; they don't even have to weigh you down. You are you for what you've been made of, and you've been made from royalty. The Creator of the Universe is on your side and what you thought was meant to harm you was actually meant for good, to transport you on to your next victory and the glory that awaits.

"But Jordan, I've had _____ and _____ happen to me, and that's why I'm not doing well, I have so many problems, I don't know if I can get back on track."

If you find yourself saying something along those lines, then we need to put this into a better perspective for you. I would advise you to take a trip to your local hospital, or even volunteer at a children's hospital. Spend some time there. I think you'll realize very quickly that your problems are insignificant.

Still having difficulty accepting that your problems are too hard to handle? Take a trip to a morgue, which is where lifeless bodies are kept to be identified. After this, I'd bet that you'll realize your problems are insignificant, if not nonexistent.

THE UNIVERSAL PERSPECTIVE

"Look again at that dot. That's here. That's home. That's us. On it everyone you love, everyone you know, everyone you ever heard of, every human being who ever was, lived out their lives. The aggregate of our joy and suffering, thousands of confident religions, ideologies, and economic doctrines, every hunter and forager, every hero and coward, every creator and destroyer of civilization, every king and peasant, every young couple in love, every mother and father, hopeful child, inventor and explorer, every teacher of morals, every corrupt politician, every "superstar," every "supreme leader," every saint and sinner in the history of our species lived there-on a mote of dust suspended in a sunbeam."

—Carl Sagan

I know the methods of putting things in perspective that we just talked about are rather gloomy, but I have a better, more powerful way to put your problems in perspective.

Whenever I feel my problems are beginning to overwhelm me, I go outside at night, lay down, and look up at the sky for 30 minutes or so. I don't know about you, but the solar system is the single most fascinating thing I have ever attempted to grasp in my mind, especially when you consider how vast and intricate it all is. Did you know that the light from stars takes multiple years to reach Earth (some take up to 900,000 years!)? The closest star's light takes four years to reach Earth, which means we are seeing it four years in the past when we look at it with our own eyes. Fascinating. Did you know that it would take 30,000 years to leave our galaxy, the Milky Way, even if we developed the technology to travel at the speed of light? Did you know that the next closest galaxy, Andromeda, is 2.5 *million* light years away (it would take 2.5 million years to get there even when traveling at the speed of light!)? Did you know that one day on Venus is the equivalent of 243 Earth days but one year on Venus is only equivalent to 224.7 Earth days? And did you know that, unlike Earth, Mercury has no atmosphere?

If you're as in awe of the universe as I am, I encourage you to go out at night and lay a blanket down. Sit out there, no phone, no music, no nothing. Just you, maybe a significant other, and the whole world right in front of you. The entire world is in front of you, quite literally.

Take it in, and you'll gain what I refer to as a Universal Perspective. Keeping this perspective is a fantastic way to live. **When you obtain the Universal Perspective, suddenly everything becomes funny, and nothing is too serious; you hardly even take yourself seriously, which is a good thing, because humility is the gateway to all other virtues.** Life becomes radically awesome. The world becomes fascinating. You become deeply curious. The people around us become unique works of art.

For me, there is no greater perspective than the one that is universal.

PROBLEMS = PROGRESS

"Every problem is a gift - without problems we would not grow."
—**Tony Robbins**

Now I'm not going to sit here and pretend that problems don't exist. We all have backpacks filled with all sorts of baggage on our backs. But I have another empowering equation for you to add to your journal:

Problems = Progress. That's a simple one. Once you understand this (we'll go into detail about it in a minute) you can effectively take your backpack full of baggage off your back, strap it to a rocket, then shoot it into the wonderfully fascinating mystery that is outer space.

How does that sound? Are you ready to be stripped of your baggage?

I know I was ready three years ago when I decided to change my life.

You see, we will all encounter a wide-ranging spectrum of problems and troubles throughout our lives, but we must never allow them to become excuses. There are two varieties of people in this world, and one believes wholeheartedly in the equation that trouble is equal to transportation, while the other variety of person is utterly ignorant of that equation. The first person believes things happen *for* them while the second person believes things happen *to* them. The first person is a creator while the second person is a victim. It is only a small change of words, but a significant difference in the quality of life that each person experiences.

BE REAL WITH YOURSELF

We all have problems. You are no different. I am no different. I just mentioned this.

I'll take it a step further by saying that one of the only things we can feel absolutely certain about is that we are going to experience these bumps in the road sometime in the near future.

We never really get rid of these problems either. Some things are always going to suck. That's reality. And the reality isn't all that bad. Allow me to put this into perspective.

Striving to achieve a life free of problems and struggle is the beginning of delusion because we don't get rid of problems. Just because you're rich or famous or have a six-pack or are the best-looking person on Earth doesn't mean your problems will magically go away like an escape artist. It doesn't work like that, and this is what so many people who are chasing after things miss. Consequently, this is why these people become more miserable after the successful completion of a significant goal.

The person who eats like crap suffers from health and image problems while the person who does eat healthy suffers from the fear of missing out (FOMO) on pizza and french fries (my weaknesses!).

Maybe you're single, and the problem is that you feel lonely and the various issues of the single life. Loneliness may indeed be a problem for some. But if you think you won't have a whole new set of problems when you meet your partner, then you may be sorely mistaking. With a newfound partner, we may now complain of not getting enough sleep at night, having to eat out too much, coming up with new date ideas each week, and if we are really delusional (and most of us are), we might complain of not having enough alone time.

There are plenty of people that simply do not have the opportunity to go to school. These peoples' problem is that they lack opportunity. But people that go to school have problems too. They complain of pointless busywork that does not apply to the real world, professors grading unfairly, and losing sleep to studying all night.

Entrepreneurs have far different problems from people who work for someone else. Vastly different, yet they both still have problems. However, I've chosen the problems of an entrepreneur because those problems are more fulfilling for me. I like the challenge. I like the struggle. I like that set of problems better.

In short:

❖The unhealthy person has problems. So does the

healthy person.

❖ The single person has problems. So does the person in a relationship.

❖ The uneducated have problems. So do the educated.

❖ People who work for someone else have problems. So do entrepreneurs.

❖ People without a dog have problems. People with dogs have problems.

❖ The poor have problems. So do the rich.

❖ Ordinary people have problems. So do famous people.

The list goes on.

Some sets of problems are better than others though. Some problems are more fulfilling than others. And the only thing we can ever do is exchange our current problems for better problems. Challenges are part of life. Knowing that we cannot evade problems, all we must do is choose which set of problems we want.

Life without problems would be boring anyway.

In any case, life ain't all sunshine and rainbows, old sport. Choose your set of problems wisely.

Believe it or not, acknowledging this gives us a sense of peace and even confidence that arises from merely knowing.

There will always be things that suck. This is a sobering truth, yet oddly useful. Don't ignore it. Don't bullshit yourself by pretending everything is sunshine and rainbows. This is a major key. All positivity all the time is straight bullshit.

I'd always wondered why my Father seemed to be cynical about life in this manner yet still seemed to be content with everything. It didn't add up. But I've come to realize that he understands the sobering truth that there will always be some things in life that suck.

This truth set him free. It set me free. It can set you free too. Gone is the pressure to make everything "perfect" and be all flustered when they aren't what you imagined. It's ok. It's inevitable. Don't be so hard on yourself.

Look in the Mirror

Along the same lines of allowing your life to be imperfect, allow yourself to be imperfect. We must look ourselves in the mirror sometimes and see what we don't want to see in order to become who we aspire to become. **We must be honest with ourselves if we ever want to improve.** But at the same time, you'll still never be perfect. **All we can do is improve. And that is freeing.**

But Everyone Else Is Perfect Though

According to who?

According to themselves on Instagram and Facebook?

That's a bit like asking a cigarette manufacturer to provide evidence that their products are safe to use, which is exactly what happened from the 1930s until the 1950s. At a time when there was no internet to find out otherwise and when solely placing trust in the hands of physicians regarding health was the norm, cigarette manufacturers provided evidence to physicians claiming cigarettes were not harmful. The manufacturers even went so far as to feature physicians in their ads to brainwash the public. Below are some headlines of ads featuring physicians from newspapers.

❖ "Not One Single Case of Throat Irritation Due to Smoking Camels"
❖ "More Doctors Smoke Camels Than Any Other Cigarette"

❖ "Give Your Throat a Vacation... Smoke a FRESH Cigarette"
❖ "20,679 Physicians Say 'Luckies' Are Less Irritating"
❖ "Science Discovered It... You Can Prove It"
❖ "NOW... 10 Months Scientific Evidence for Chesterfield"
❖ "Just What the Doctor Ordered"
❖ "Chesterfield Best for You"
❖ "Why Physicians Call Our New Brand "A HEALTH CIGAR"

Do you really believe that stuff?

Well, the American public did for more than twenty years until they finally caught on. Now everyone knows cigarettes cause fatal lung cancer and all sorts of negative health externalities.

In similar fashion, people post Instagram pictures and Facebook status updates to show and tell everyone how *amazing* their life is even though many of them are depressed. This creates a skewed image of the world. It creates delusion. If you want to believe in that skewed image, be delusional, and put the pressure on yourself to be as "perfect" as everyone else, then feel free. I'm not stopping you. It may be an endless pursuit that results in misery, however.

Just as the American public caught on to cigarettes being unhealthy, I think we are beginning to catch on to the façade that others put up. I think we are beginning to realize that peoples' lives aren't as perfect as they hype it up to be. I hope I'm right about this.

TRUST THE PROCESS

"Trust the process"
—A mantra synonymous with the culture of the Philadelphia 76ers

"What doesn't kill you makes you stronger" might be the most cliché statement out there but it is 100 percent true. Every successful person I know has gone through some sort of adversity. It was part of their journey by default. **Adversity is the prerequisite to success.**

Let's say you, and everyone else, can easily lift 100 pounds when you go to the gym. You and everyone else who goes to the gym does it every day for three months. Let's say 100 pounds is easy for everyone. Then, one day, for no reason at all, the gym's crazy manager (we'll call her Unreasonable Olga) makes a new rule that you can only lift 300 pounds now. It's unreasonable, it's unfair, and you don't understand why it must be like this. Some gym-goers cancel their membership at the gym as soon as this happens. They're not in the game anymore. They quit. But you? You stayed because even though you might not understand why this had to happen to you, you trusted that it would make you stronger. The new 300-pound rule stays intact for five months. In month one, you couldn't lift the 300 pounds at all, but you attempted. In month two, you made progress. You lifted it one time. By month three, you lifted it a few more times. A month later, you get a few more repetitions in. By the end of month five, you can bang out a set of ten repetitions with ease. You've *adapted* to the change, *developed* resilience, and you've *grown* mentally and physically. Then our crazy manager, Unreasonable Olga, decides to abolish the 300-pound rule. So, you go back to lifting 100 pounds, and you find that it is way too easy. There's no challenge. You aren't being stimulated enough. Then you start lifting 200 pounds. 200 pounds gives you a modest challenge, but you know you can do more, so you go up to 250 pounds, and that's just right.

After getting wind that the 300-pound rule has been abolished, the gym-goers that canceled their membership immediately after the rule was put in place come crawling back. They try lifting 100 pounds but find it's too hard now, so they go down to 80 pounds. **They aren't as strong as they used to be because they decided to quit when things got tough. They didn't trust the process. They didn't care to use empowering questions to search for a deeper meaning, which would have been that they could come out stronger.**

What am I saying?

I mean that you can't just quit when things get tough. Don't withdraw yourself from the opportunity to get stronger, wiser, and to grow in all areas of your life. I'm asking you to keep the faith, trusting that there is a deeper meaning behind the adversity and that it will lead you on to your next victory in life. Can you keep the faith for me?

Sometimes it feels like we have to walk around carrying 300 pounds worth of challenges we don't want. But that's part of the journey. It's part of the process. Will you trust it?

By carrying that 300 pounds, you'll grow into the best version of yourself.

In my own life, I know I wouldn't have been able to accomplish all I have without going through all I've gone through. Clearly, I didn't understand why I was suffering from depression at the time. None of it made sense. I thought it wasn't fair and that everyone else in the world had it better than me. I was jealous of the popular kids. I wished I was them. It seemed like their lives were perfect; they were good-looking, and they always had dates to homecoming and prom and were invited to parties.

But you know what's funny?

Many of them peaked in high school. Yep, I said it. They peaked. They missed out on adversity, so they never grew. Meanwhile, I had a hefty dose of adversity and I grew because of it. Adversity forced me to become my best self and to do it quickly, or else I was probably running out of time before I would have eventually just ended my life. My level of necessity was high. Everything was a must. I had to seek out new resources, build new skills, and get out of the damn comfort zone that silently almost killed me. I had to take new actions, actions that I hadn't done previously because if I kept doing the same thing, I would have kept getting the same thing. **I knew that I could predict what the next few years of life would look like if I didn't take a new action immediately ... the next few years would have looked ... the ... same.**

I didn't want that. So, I built my lifestyle from the ground up and blazed my trail.

High school was a time in my life of intense anxiety, immense pressure, and crippling fear.

Looking back on everything, I don't think I should have felt fearful because I had nothing to lose; If you're ever going through a tough time, I think that's an excellent question to ask (what do you have to lose?), because the answer is nothing. Then go a bit further by asking yourself, "What do I have to gain?", to which the answer will almost always be a resounding *EVERYTHING!*

Wrapping this story up and putting a bow on it, let me tell you exactly what I have to say about the adversity I faced along my journey.

1. Without it, there is a 0.0 percent chance that this book would exist, a 0.0 percent chance that I would

be a 20-year-old entrepreneur, and a 0.0 percent chance that I would have found any purpose in life, which currently is to grow each day and to empower you to grow with me. My quality of life would be no higher than average and I wouldn't be the happy soul I am.

2. I wouldn't trade my adversity for the world ... it is the best thing that has ever happened to me; it is my most prized possession.

Trust that there is a deeper meaning in every challenge. Trust that the trouble is transporting you to your next victory and beyond to become your best self.

And I'll leave you with this: You can change your life any day you wish. All you must do is take a new action. Take that new action, and your life will explode into change. You won't regret it.

At this point, the only thing that matters is how you live the rest of your life.

"The past is a place of reference, not a place of residence."
—Roy T. Bennet

OPEN TO INTERPRETATION

"We can not solve our problems with the same level of thinking that created them."
—Albert Einstein

For most of my life, I would feel devastated whenever I got dumped. It happened every time without failure, no matter the length of the relationship. That first time I got dumped in high school, I fell into an unnecessary multi-year depression. Every relationship that ended after that still put me in dark places emotionally, although it never lasted more than a month or two. However, in my most recent relationships, I've wised up to something funny, and that is the fact that all events are neutral. **Events are not inherently positive or negative by nature. What makes these events positive or negative is the way we interpret the events. Meaning matters most. And we will never heal from any troublesome event unless we change the meaning that we attach to it.**

When I used to get dumped, my interpretation was this: I'm not good enough, this doesn't make sense, being single sucks, I'll never find a good relationship, why me.

When I get dumped nowadays, my interpretation is this: This means I get to explore, this means I get to grow, this means that this person simply was not meant for me, this was not a divine connection, there is better out there for me, this trouble is transporting me to my next victory, being single means I have more time to search for the best version of myself, this means I have more time to read, this means I have more time to learn, this means I have more time!

Clearly, the latter interpretation is far more empowering. Empowering interpretations can be applied to any and every event in your life. If someone close to you dies, you can interpret it in one of two ways: 1) Why did this have to happen? Life will suck without this person, or 2) I have an angel watching over me.

"We can complain because rose bushes have thorns, or rejoice because thorns have roses."
—Alphonse Karr

If you get fired from your job, you can interpret it in one of two ways: 1) This means I'm going to struggle for money, this sucks, the pressure is on, or 2) This is my big chance to find and begin the work of my life, this means I have an opportunity to find new work that empowers me to empower others, this means I am going to learn how to manage my money better, this was not meant for my harm, this was meant for my good, I trust that I am coming out stronger and more prosperous.

Creating more empowering meanings behind things allows us to embrace adversity, handle it like a champ, be more stable, and trust the process by default. We may not be able to control what happens to us, but we can always control the meaning an event holds. When trouble means transportation to you, your life explodes into change.

HOW TO RESPOND TO TRAGEDY

Let me be clear that I'm not asking you to be a senseless robot when bad things happen. I believe not allowing yourself to *feel* is unhealthy. Instead, connect with your emotions, but trust the process at the same time. When you do this, you'll experience the full spectrum of your emotions, which enables you to realize just how precious the good times are in life. And by allowing yourself to feel pain and brokenness while trusting the process, you open the door to growth. I call this *Quality Suffering.*

GOLDEN REPAIR

Kintsukuroi (golden repair) is a Japanese method of repairing broken pottery with lacquer mixed with either gold, silver, or platinum. When pottery breaks, the Japanese don't just render it useless and throw it away as Americans would. Instead, they see breakage as something that adds to the history, value, beauty, and uniqueness of an object. It's not something they try to hide, as they make the filled-in cracks noticeably shiny.

In the same way, we as humans should not be rendered useless when we break (and we all do). Sadly, some are not aware of the high power this concept wields, and this is why we have suicides. **When we break, it is not permanent. We must trust that adversity is what makes us unique. We must trust that it is adding to our history, value, and overall beauty.**

PRINCIPLE 6:

Start viewing setbacks as setups and trouble as transportation.

Chapter Resources: Black hole size comparison video, The smallest thing to the biggest thing in the universe video, 76ers trust the process article, Tom Brady's story: why adversity is a gift video.

JordanParisHealth.com/gmu-backpack

CHAPTER 7

AWAKEN YOUR POTENTIAL

"There comes a time when you ought to start doing what you want. Take a job that you love. You will jump out of bed in the morning. I think you are out of your mind if you keep taking jobs that you don't like because you think it will look good on your resume. Isn't that a little like saving up sex for your old age?"
—WARREN BUFFETT

GROWTH

MINDSET

UNIVERSITY

The caterpillar is quite an interesting species.

It is born as a creepy crawler and proceeds to eat a ton, get fat, and double in size over a matter of days. Next, it goes away to a dark place for a while, staying in one place all alone. Then, in a sort of shock and remarkable turn of events, a beautiful butterfly that resembles nothing of its former self emerges from the dark cocoon and flies off to explore the world, find a mate, reproduce, and die happy.

Humans are much the same way. We are born. We crawl around in misery for some time. We eat a ton, get fat, and double in size (over a matter of days?!). Next, we go away for a little while, we work on ourselves, preparing for the next phase of life. Then, in a sort of shock and remarkable turn of events, a well-rounded, successful, fulfilled, high-flying human being that resembles nothing of our former selves emerges from the darkness and goes on to break the poverty of our previously poor mindset, explore the world, create reality, find a partner, reproduce, and die happy.

But there's only one problem: Many of us don't make it out of the cocoon, that dark place. We are miserable. So, we go away. But many of us don't leave that dark place. Some people do end up making it out of that dark place though, and they go on to fulfill their potential that lies in the rest of their life cycle. Often, the ones that stay trapped in their cocoon for a lifetime are the ones who don't believe wholeheartedly in their dreams or even themselves, and they care all too much about what everyone else says or thinks about them. On the contrary, the ones that make it out are the ones that believe in themselves, believe in their dreams, and go for it all without giving a fuck about what anyone else says or thinks. The ones that make it out have a growth mindset.

HAPPENINGS

We've already established that everyone has excuses. We've all had things happen to us. Happenings are common occurrences.

But It's not about what happens to us; it's about what we do about what happens to us.

What happens usually happens to all of us. For example, the sun set on all of us last night. It was a somewhat common occurrence. The sun rose the next morning, another common occurrence. It rained on the other people around you too yesterday, yet another common occurrence.

I think it's funny how one person can wake up, see the rain and mutter, "Ugh, what a gloomy day. I'll just stay home today.", and this person allows the rain to dictate his life. On the contrary, another person can wake up, see the rain, smile and say, "Oh wow! Rain! What a glorious day to go out and crush it!", and this person goes joyfully through the day experiencing success no matter if it is raining or if the sun is out. The second person chose a different meaning about the rain, a common occurrence that happened to all of us, than the first person.

Happenings are the same, what people do is different.

My teacher, Jim Rohn, puts it this way: "I used to blame the weather. Then I discovered it rains on the rich."

Often, I reflect on a book I read many years ago called *The Other Wes Moore* by Wes Moore. It's about two kids that grew up in the same poor area, in the same time period, and they had the same name. What's interesting is that one Wes Moore ended up in prison for robbing a bank and manslaughter, while the other went on to write two books, become a social entrepreneur, television producer, political analyst, and decorated US Army officer.

Surely by now, you understand that it's not what happens, it's about how you respond to what happens.

RAISE YOUR PRICE!

Alright, before we go any further in this book, we need to understand that we'll never awaken our highest potential without raising the price of our joy. Here's what I mean by that:

Some people walk around with the price of their joy so low that anyone can afford to take it, or even steal it. They sweat the smallest of stuff, which steals their joy and lands them firmly in a perpetual suffering state. Why is this so important?

Because nobody produces outstanding results in suffering states. In suffering states, the mind's flow is severely inhibited; I know because I used to be in a perpetual suffering state. I would let the stupidest things steal my joy, like if someone said something to me, or if someone didn't say something to me (crazy, I know); It was a lose-lose scenario that perpetually disrupted my mind's flow.

Now I know better. I've learned to transcend my expectation into appreciation. While I still expect the best from myself and live by design, I drop all expectations I have of others. I neither expect something nor nothing. I am neutral. With this small change in philosophy, going from being expectant of others to dependent upon myself, I have effectively raised the price of my joy through the roof. Now, nobody can afford it, and I live in joyous states most of the time, which allows me to awaken my highest potential to produce outstanding results in my relationships, business, and life.

Don't let your joy be cheap.

WHAT'S YOUR DREAM?

"Somebody should tell us, right at the start of our lives, that we are dying. Then we might live life to the limit, every minute of every day. Do it! I say. Whatever you want to do, do it now! There are only so many tomorrows."
—Pope Paul IV

We all have dreams. They were placed in our hearts to be able to direct our lives. Don't ignore it. The dream isn't silly. It's there for a reason. I know that you know what dream I'm talking about. Maybe you gave up on it a long time ago and settled for something less. But the dream is still alive. You can always go after it. What do you have to lose? After all, every one of us is going to die eventually.

"Well, _____ and _____ could happen if I fail and I may never recover."

Remember the Universal Perspective?

Well, allow me to put this into that perspective for you. Humans have existed for about 6 million years, albeit in a primitive state, but more modern-day humans have existed for 200,000 years, I believe. Earth has been around for 4.543 billion years. NASA estimates that the age of the universe is about 13.77 billion years, but I bet that number is much higher (maybe infinite?). 100 billion galaxies have been discovered, but that number will likely double with improvements in telescope technology (also infinite?). The central black hole of Phoenix Cluster, a galaxy, is the size of 20 billion suns. Now

I'm going off topic, but you get the point. Oh, and the average human lives only 79 years. We are here for 79 out of the 4.543 billion years that Earth has existed, which roughly translates to, "Who the fuck cares if you mess up?"

If you mess up, it's barely even a blip on the radar. Remember, trouble is transportation anyway.

My point is this: **Just do it. Whatever you've been dreaming about, go for it. There are only so many tomorrows.**

Everybody walks around like they're hot stuff pretending that the stakes are so high that they couldn't possibly risk their finances or "reputation" by going after big dreams. When in reality, none of us are hot stuff and the stakes are so unbelievably low that we cannot even comprehend how low they are.

Do you want to know what high stakes are?

Andromeda, our neighboring galaxy, is set to collide head-on with our galaxy in about 4 billion years. The world (as we know it) won't even exist anymore. Those are high stakes for an entire galaxy.

So, let's get after it. Those dreams weren't put in your heart just to tease you. They're real, and they're waiting to be created by you.

"Those who mind don't matter, and those who matter don't mind."
—Dr. Seuss

PRINCIPLE 7:

Put the excuses aside and get after your dreams *today*. Decide, without hesitation.

Chapter Resources: Excuses video with Jim Rohn.

JordanParisHealth.com/gmu-backpack

CHAPTER 8

DESIGN A LIFE

"If you don't design your own life plan, chances are you'll fall into someone else's plan. And guess what they have planned for you? Not much."
—Jim Rohn

GROWTH

MINDSET

UNIVERSITY

I strive to design a life that I don't need a vacation from.

Often, people can't wait until the weekend. They lament every other day of the week that is not included in the weekend. These people can't wait for their next vacation. In fact, they wait 51 weeks desperate for their one week vacation. And I find it humorous that these people plan these vacations better than they plan the order of their entire lives. But their lack of planning is precisely the reason they find themselves lamenting weekdays, starving for the next vacation, and quite frankly, waiting for life to be over. They live in perpetual mediocrity and even misery while complaining of feeling "burnt out."

They are entirely oblivious to the fact that they're only feeling burnt out because they don't enjoy what they do. These people say they are "busy". This is called work. On the contrary, there are plenty of outstanding individuals who have creatively and effectively designed lives in which they love what they do. These people say they are *productive*. This is called purpose. In a life where we love what we do and we have a clear purpose, there is no such thing as burnout.

Like most other prosperities in life, this sort of love and purpose doesn't come without intentional design and deliberate planning. In this chapter, we'll learn the key aspects of designing a life filled with love and purpose.

PROGRAM OR BE PROGRAMMED

The world can be a very negative place. We cannot leave the wellbeing of our minds to chance. Our mind will believe everything it hears. We must feed it with wisdom, inspiration, truth, and love. We must ground ourselves firmly into the roots of these things. To do this, I suggest listening to an inspiring or educational podcast, a TED Talk, or even upbeat music as you embark upon your day. You can do this as you get dressed, while eating breakfast, or in the car on your way to work; you don't have to find time for this because you already have the time. My personal favorite way to ground myself is to read ten pages when I wake up, which takes about twenty minutes but works wonders. Then I listen to a podcast as I get ready for the day. Don't check email, texts, or social media for the first hour of the day. Don't let whatever brain candy that happens to pop up first dictate your day.

Create your own unique morning routine that embodies what you stand for. Find something that supports your cause, do it first thing in the morning, then go out in the world to advance that cause.

Wake up, drink your damn passion, then create shit. Simple.

FRONTLOADED STRESS

I want to live a good life. So do you. We share this basic intention. **For some people, the path to the good life ends at merely wishing for it. They do the things that make them feel *good in the moment* without thinking of potential ramifications down the road. Their vision is so cloudy that they can't see more than two feet in front of their faces (or two minutes).**

For example, eating chocolate lava cake feels *terrific* in the moment but it freaking sucks when you have to deal with a bulging stomach, nausea, and feeling crappy about yourself ten minutes later. You already regret eating the cake. Fuck.

The next day, you are faced with a decision: you can go out with your friends and have more cake, or you can stay in and finish that project that is due in two days. You decide to put the project off and go out and have more cake. I smell trouble.

The next day, you are faced with another decision: you can get the project done, or you can "relax" and scroll through Instagram, Facebook, and watch TV (a.k.a. the Income Reduction Box) all day and get the project done first thing in the morning. You choose the latter. Then, your friends ask if you want to go out and get hammered at the local degenerate bar. Your crush is going to be there, so you go to the local degenerate bar. You went out, and you had a good time. All is well, right? At the moment, yes.

The next morning, you wake up hungover, tired, fat, and with an unfinished project due in three hours. Yikes. You are extremely stressed. Now, you claim to be suffering from anxiety, when in reality all that happened was that you made a handful of poor decisions upstream that landed you in a stressful situation.

(Side note: Many people who claim to suffer from "anxiety" are just chronic poor decision-makers that consistently land themselves in stressful situations as a result of their poor decisions. No, I'm not insensitive to those who suffer from real anxiety. I know people who have real anxiety that pops up for no reason. I have a friend that has real anxiety. I understand. Just be wary of people who complain of "anxiety," because many times they are the creators of it in the first place, not the victims.)

This is called *Backloaded Stress*. Backloaded Stress happens when people fall for the lure of feeling good in the

moment while simultaneously sacrificing their wellbeing and sovereignty in the future.

Backloaded Stress is when you do the things that are easy today, which consequently makes your life hard tomorrow.

The opposite is referred to as *Frontloaded Stress*. Frontloaded Stress happens when you sacrifice pleasure in the moment in an effort to invest in your future prosperity.

Frontloaded stress is when you do the things that are hard today because you know that doing these things today will make your life easy tomorrow.

Backloaded Stress = a mess.

Frontloaded Stress = success.

An example of frontloaded stress would be sitting down to write that book or finish that project you know you should be working on instead of scrolling through social media.

Laying in bed, whipping out the phone, and scrolling through social media is so easy to do. On the contrary, sitting down to write that book or finish that project is an arduous, long, and difficult process. But guess what? Doing the latter is going to make your life much easier tomorrow. It might even make it more enjoyable.

In a world where the vast majority of people are out partying, getting hammered, stoned, doing nothing productive, and scrolling through social media all day (a.k.a. backloading stress), you have an unbelievable opportunity to get ahead, to accomplish things in a matter of months that would take the majority years or even decades to accomplish. You have an opportunity to make your life easy tomorrow by simply choosing to do the more difficult things today.

This concept is simple, and you can use it to produce outstanding results in your life once you have a keen grasp of it.

"Well," you say, "Jordan, if this is so easy, then how come everyone doesn't do it?"

Excellent question.

Everyone doesn't do this because they do not understand this concept and because this concept is very easy not to implement; laying in bed is easy. Scrolling through social media is easy. Going out to party every night is easy. Not going to the gym is easy. Not reading ten pages per day is easy. Eating like crap is easy. It's a whole bunch of easy. Doing the easy stuff is easy. But it's not as easy to do the not-so-easy stuff.

So, the majority chooses to do what's easy, which pits them firmly in an endless loop of backloaded stress, anxiety, poor results, and the reality of a hopelessly average life.

The ones that are aware of the pitfalls and take advantage of this loop are life's champions. These are the world-beaters. And their lives are much easier than those in the majority, the ones who do the easy stuff.

The Master of Frontloaded Stress

My Father. That's him—The Master of Frontloaded Stress. The man who says, "If you look up 'Delayed Gratification' in the dictionary, a picture of my face shows up." He consistently chose to stay up late to study, even on weekends, over the lure of a wild college frat party. The fact that he lived in the frat house itself makes the feat that much more impressive. The parties would have been a ton of fun, for sure. It would have been easy to party. But he understood the principle of Frontloaded Stress: Do the hard stuff today to make life easy tomorrow. He mastered it. He graduated near the top of his class in high school, at Emory University, and wherever else he graduated from. He went to school until he was 30 with the goal of becoming a doctor. He didn't get to take the job as a surgeon until he was in his thirties, while many of his peers settled for average jobs ten years prior. My Father always chose to get the tough stuff out of the way, knowing there would be a reward in the future. Now 53, let's just say he lives the good life, an easier life than most.

LIVE WITH INTENTION, BY DESIGN

When do I start my day? After I've designed it.

When do I embark on a new goal? After I've designed and planned out what I need to achieve that goal.

When do I walk into a meeting? After I've set the intention for it.

When do I begin anything in my life? After I've decided what it will take for me to have a level ten experience.

When do I begin to live my best life? After I've designed it.

You see, going through life with our fingers crossed is one of those *easy* things to do. It's easy to not design your life and set intention in the moment. But this way of living is 100 percent dependent upon luck and other bullshit that shouldn't dictate your life. But this is precisely what happens when all we do is cross our fingers and hope for the best. Sometimes luck is on our side. Unfortunately, it usually is not.

Fortunately for you and me, there is a better way; **we can creatively and effectively design our lives.**

If you're one of my loyal Instagram followers (isn't it taboo to talk about your social media?!), you may have noticed the quote I've had in my bio section for about two years straight now. It says, "Don't make a living, design a life!" (ok, stalkers, I added the exclamation point only last year.)

Well, that quote sure sounds nice, huh?

It sure does.

But (contrary to popular belief) this is not the reason it has stuck with me as my motto for the entirety of my adult life.

It stuck because it has real meaning to it. It stuck because this is actually how I live my life. It stuck because it got me out of depression. It stuck because it helped me achieve things in a matter of months that takes people who just cross their fingers years or even eternity to accomplish. It stuck because it worked. That's why.

Only Dead Fish Go with the Flow

I'm talking to a woman I've never met before. We're getting to know each other. It's going well.

"I'm really just a go with the flow kind of person," she says.

I hear this *all the time.*

And that's the exact moment I become turned off. 100 to zero real quick. People who "go with the flow" aren't really my type of people. That's' just my personal preference. I can enjoy their presence, and I can have fun with them, but nothing more than that. I find it much more challenging to have intellectual conversations and form meaningful relationships with "go with the flow" people. Allow me to explain why this is.

The types of people that I can align visions with and the ones I can form meaningful relationships with are *usually* the ones that consciously direct the flow of their own lives. They don't have their fingers crossed. They don't rely on wishful thinking. Instead, they are creators of their reality. They are the captains of their ship. They are the masters of their fate. These are the world-beaters, the world-class high performers. These are the types of people I surround myself with.

If you want to achieve success and live a good life, then you might want to consider captaining your ship. This way you won't get caught up in the flow of the *current, current* events, *current* fears, *current* desires, and *current* circumstances. You won't get swept away.

The truth is, many of the problems we face today could have been prevented by better decision-making upstream. Instead, most of us choose to go with the flow and only realize there's a real problem when it's too late. And by that time, we've gone with the flow so long that there is no going back because we've already fallen over the waterfall and into the pit of misery, stress, and "anxiety."

When you go with the flow, you let things happen to you as opposed to taking control of your life and creating your reality. So, unless you want to be controlled by the current, don't go with the flow. Direct the flow.

Below are vital principles of living with intention, by design.

❖ Don't wait for things to happen, make things happen.

❖ Don't hope for change, create change.

❖ Don't wait for the right people to talk to you, talk to the right people.

❖ Don't go with the flow, direct the flow.

❖ Don't wait for the stars to align, align the stars.

❖ Don't wait to be happy to smile, smile to be happy.

❖ Don't jump into the deep end, then figure it out. Figure it out, then jump into the deep end.

❖ Don't get in front of an audience, then decide what to say. Decide what to say, then get in front of an audience.

❖ Don't wait for inspiration and ideas to begin writing. Begin writing for inspiration and ideas.

❖ Don't let reality create you. Create reality.

❖ Don't let fate be your master, be the master of your fate.

❖ Don't make a living, design a life.

DESIGNING GOALS – THIS IS WHAT DREAMS ARE MADE OF

"The only thing standing between you and your goal is the bullshit story you keep telling yourself as to why you can't achieve it."
—Jordan Belfort

Dream big. But start small. Then connect the dots. Keep it going.

Sounds simple, right?

Good news: it is.

Dream Big

What are your goals?

What are your dreams?

What is it that you want in this world?

What do you want to experience?

Where do you want to go?

If you could have life any way you liked, what would it look like?

Whenever I want something, I decide what I want. I write it down.

Start Small

It's not easy to make a bunch of changes all at once, and that's ok.

Start small. Sometimes the big picture can be overwhelming. Let's just take this decision by decision, making small changes. Over time, these small changes add up to make a big difference because the way you change your life is by making one good decision after another.

This is how I changed my life and even my eating habits.

I started small. Nothing happened overnight. I remember being 12 or 13 years old when I made the decision to limit my soda consumption to once per month. So, I had that one soda per month for a while (maybe six months) until I just stopped having it completely without even realizing it. The neural pathway in my brain that once craved soda 24/7 withered, and the disempowering behavior (drinking soda) disappeared with it.

Then I started making more small changes, one at a time:

❖ I decided to eat a vegetable at one meal per day, and so I worked on that for a while.

❖ I decided to eat organic foods as much as possible, and so I worked on that for a while.

❖ I decided to have a green shake every morning, and so I worked on that for a while.

❖ I decided to cut added sugar out of my diet, and so I worked on that for a while.

❖ I decided to go against the grain, eliminating grains from my diet, and so I worked on that for a while.

❖ I decided to limit my meat consumption to once or twice per month, and so I worked on that for a while.

❖ I decided to stop drinking water out of plastic, and I'm working on that now.

The bottom line: start small, don't put the unnecessary pressure on yourself to be perfect starting right now. Changing my eating habits was a long process that I didn't put too much effort towards. Nonetheless, I started small, made continual progress, and ended up mastering healthy eating over half a decade.

In a similar (but much speedier) fashion, we can achieve our goals and develop new skills by mapping out a step by step path to getting what we want. Each decision I made to become healthier was just a simple step.

Whenever I want something, I figure out what I need to do to make it happen. I write it down in steps (usually three to ten steps). **Once I know my steps, I work on one step at a time, I rarely get distracted, and I have peace of mind understanding the clear path. It makes getting what you want really freaking easy.**

For example, when I wanted to become an elite internet entrepreneur that actually helps people, this was my step by step process.

1. Build a radically awesome website. To be an internet entrepreneur, I must have a website. Duh. Obvious first step. Nothing else works without this.
2. Start writing blog posts at least once per week to build SEO and attract an audience.
3. Create an automated email series for subscribers and future program buyers.
4. Build an email list.
5. Create programs to offer to my email list and the rest of the internet.
6. Appear in a major media outlet.
7. Offer free stuff to get more emails.
8. Create more programs.
9. Write a book.

It's worth mentioning that I also had a separate step by step process for launching this book, *which I was able to write in 29 days and publish in another few weeks because of the laser-*

guided focus provided by my clearly identified steps. Two months, one full book. I did it. I'm not special. You can do it too. It takes most authors years to write this much because they don't have clearly identified steps, or even a purpose that acts as a gravitational pull toward the successful completion of a book.

When I wanted to become a personal trainer, all I had to do was figure out the steps I would need to execute to carry out this plan. These were my steps for making this happen. Any activity that didn't involve these steps was considered a distraction.

1. Find a mentor to learn from who is doing what I want to do. Reach out to that person and go work for that person for free.
2. Get the best certification.
3. Build an awesome website and start blogging.
4. Attract clients through guerilla marketing and various apps that allow clients to discover and reach out to me.

Another one of my goals is to give a TED Talk within the next two years. Here is my step by step path for this.

1. Develop masterful public speaking skills by reading books on the topic, including *TED Talks: The Official TED Guide to Public Speaking,* and by studying the best public speakers.
2. Develop my idea worth sharing. I can't give a TED Talk if I have nothing of value to talk about.
3. Write a book to build credibility.
4. Find other speaking opportunities to build more

credibility.

5. Connect with, reach out, and offer value to TEDx hosts and TED speakers on LinkedIn. I must go above and beyond by nurturing and leveraging my connections.

6. Be invited or apply to speak at a TED event.

Now that I just told you that this is a goal I'm after, I will look foolish if I don't follow through. I've effectively raised my level of necessity by sharing my goal with you. I've been sharing my goals with friends for years, and I've found that doing so holds me accountable for what I say I'm going to do.

You can do this for just about any goal or dream that you have in your heart. I prefer to write down this step by step process for at least one short-term goal (under one year), one mid-term goal (one to three years), and one long-term goal (three to ten years). Once I have it all written down, I know exactly what I need to do to achieve each one. Then I spend a majority of my time focusing on the steps while categorizing everything else as a distraction. **No wishful thinking, just living by design. This is how you make things happen.**

Connect the Dots

Don't skip steps. Don't bounce back and forth between steps. Just work on one at a time, allowing discipline to be the bridge between each step. As I just said, once you've mapped out how you are going to get what you want in a step by step path, all that is left to do is simply connect the dots, or simply walk up the steps laid out in front of you. But **we need the steps to be able to climb.**

Keep it Going – Don't Outrun Your Dream

When we were discussing the inevitability of problems earlier, we explored why some people achieve all of their goals and reach the top of the mountain yet still feel miserable. The first reason is that they expect that all their problems will magically disappear when they make it to the top, which we know is untrue.

Another factor that contributes to the sad feeling even after achieving whatever they wanted to achieve is the fact that they simply outran their goals and neglected to set any new ones.

They achieved X, Y, and Z, then they said, "That's it, I did it. Now I'm done." But that's not how it works. Our brains are wired for growth. We can't just stop. **Once we think we've done it all, once we stop growing, we begin to die; there is nothing else to live for, nothing that pulls us out of bed in the morning.** At this point, life sucks.

We must have new goals to go after, new projects to work on, new skills to develop. Life is boring without new stimuli. **As soon as we are about to achieve a significant goal, we must design the next set of goals.**

Most importantly, we should have a forever goal, an intangible process-oriented goal that magnetically inspires us every single day and never expires. My forever goal is this: Magnetically inspire others by being relentlessly consistent.

My forever goal inspires me, guides my interactions, and influences my every waking moment.

Goal-Designing Workshop

You probably could have guessed this was coming when I said that I write all this stuff down! Now, I apologize in advance for incorporating a cheesy goal workshop into this book. I didn't want to do it, but it's an absolutely essential practice for anyone that wants to create lasting change in their lives. Anyway, we're going to do this to help you get some clarity in your life. It'll be fun. Like learning to ride a bike.

Fun fact: When I was learning to ride a bike in my driveway as a four-year-old, I said, "I can't do it" about 100 times as I cried. Meanwhile, I was biking around the driveway perfectly, like a pro.

The same may happen as we design our goals together. You may say you can't do it and cry about it, but I have confidence that you will still get the job done effectively.

Let's dive in, shall we?

1. Get a separate sheet of paper, a notebook, or your journal.

2. **Dream Big** – Write down a collection of about 30-50 goals and place a timeline next to each one (ex. three months, one year, four years, etc.). They could be contribution goals, material goals, career goals, places you want to go, people you want to meet, sights you want to see, places you want to live, the money you want to make, the car you want, or anything else your heart desires. Don't hold back. What do you want? Once finished, circle your most important short-term goal (under one year), your most important mid-term goal (one to three years), and your most important long-term goal (three to ten years).

3. **Start Small** – With the three most important goals that you circled, develop a three to ten step path you need to follow to achieve each goal. What are the major things that must get done to achieve each goal?

4. **Connect the Dots** – Now you know what must be done. You have clarity. Dedicate most of your time to the steps you've written out. Momentum is yours to create.

5. **Keep it Going** – Set a forever goal that inspires you, guides your interactions, and influences your every waking moment.

CREATE YOUR BRAND OF AWESOME

"We can change our lives. We can do, have, and be exactly what we wish."
—Tony Robbins

All of us are walking, talking brands, whether we realize it consciously or not.

What's beautiful about the power of design is that not only can we design our lives, but we can design ourselves. We can design our entire persona. We can be who we want to be, and we can do what we want to do because our identity influences our actions. We will always find ways to support our identity through our actions. Our values, inspiration, and purpose should be aligned with who we believe our best future self to be. When shaping identity, which I call creating your own brand of awesome, consider the following questions:

1. What kind of person typically achieves what I want to achieve or lives the life I want to live?
2. What level of thinking would it take for me to rise to this level?
3. What values would my best self hold?
4. What values should my best self start moving away from?
5. How would my best self walk, talk, think, act, and even breathe?
6. When my five closest friends describe me ten years

from now, I would want them to say things like...

Align Person with Persona

We all know that guy who tries to act cool around certain people. They walk with this sort of cocky swagger when they think others are watching. The problem doesn't lie in the walk necessarily, but in the fact that this person isn't the same person in private as they are in public. This is a common character flaw. However, **one of the greatest signs of maturity is when someone's persona in public is the same as the person they are in private, the person they truly are.** When designing yourself, ensure this sort of alignment is intact.

Principle 8: Don't go with the flow, direct the flow; Don't make a living, design a life.

Chapter Resources: My perfectly designed day video.

JordanParisHealth.com/gmu-backpack

PHASE 3

INSPIRE

"Good actions give strength to ourselves and inspire good actions in others."
—Plato

CHAPTER 9

GROW TO GIVE

"We make a living by what we get. We make a life by what we give."
—Winston Churchill

GROWTH

MINDSET

UNIVERSITY

Once upon a time, there was a tree that loved a boy.

The boy would visit the tree every day to play, to climb, to swing on the branches, to gather up the leaves, and to eat the tree's apples. They even played hide and seek together. The boy and the tree loved each other very much, which made the tree happy.

As the boy grew older, he slowly began to stop spending as much time with the tree. The tree invites him to play, but he declines because all he wants is money. So, the tree tells him to pick the apples to sell to the city for money. He does that, which makes the tree happy.

Much time passes until the boy, now a man, comes back to visit again, but when he finally does, he declines to play with the tree because all he wants is a house. So, the tree tells the boy to cut off its branches to build a house. He does that, which makes the tree happy.

The boy has grown into an older man by the next time he visits. Again, the tree invites him to play, but the boy declines because he is sad and all he wants is a boat so he can get away. So, the tree tells the boy to cut down its trunk to make a boat to get away with. He does that, but the tree isn't as happy as before because it has nothing left to give.

The boy returns once more. By now, he has grown into his elder years. The tree apologizes for having nothing to give, but the boy says all he wants is a quiet place to sit and rest. The tree is delighted to offer its stump. The boy sits down to rest, and the tree is happy.

"And the tree was happy"
—Shel Silverstein, The Giving Tree

This is the story of *The Giving Tree*, beautifully told by Shel Silverstein. This book was an essential part of my childhood, as my mother and father read it to me as a bedtime story on countless occasions. At first glance, it may seem to be a sad story that leaves us feeling sorry for the tree. That's what I used to think, but as I've reflected upon this story over the course of my life, I believe it is not so sad. Instead, it teaches us a valuable lesson: **sincere and selfless contribution is what enables us to experience true fulfillment.**

The tree never stopped giving, to the point where it was left with nothing, yet it ended up happy and fulfilled. The boy, who gave nothing and was on the receiving end of the tree's gifts for an entire lifetime, endured a life of sadness and misery even though he seemingly had it all (money, a partner, a house, a boat). From Shel's beautifully told story, we learn that **it's not about what we get; it's about what we give.**

In the same way, continual growth and development should not always be about what we get. It should not always be about the wealth we will get. It should not always be about the attention we will get. It should not always be about how great we will become. Make no mistake, those are all great, but they are not what matters most.

What matters most is about what we give, what we contribute to society, the lives we positively influence, the human beings we uplift along our journey. That's what matters. Giving is the prerequisite for fulfillment.

Wait a Minute ... Is Giving Selfish?

Numerous psychological studies have claimed that humans are selfish by nature. This explains why we ditch our friends at the bar to hook up with someone, why we write our names down first on a group project, why we dish out a bit more food for ourselves (except for mothers!), and so on. We try to tip the scale in our favor if we think it will make us happier. However, this isn't always a bad thing.

If we know that giving will make us happy, then it makes sense that we will be more likely to give to others, even if we do so for selfish reasons. This means that the act of giving may not be selfless, but that's ok.

"For it is in giving that we receive."
—St. Francis of Assisi

In an odd way, my faith in humanity comes from knowing that humans are selfish because humans that have experienced what it feels like to give will keep repeating the process, giving to others, increasing the value of others, helping others along.

WHAT'S THE POINT OF LIFE?

"Live to learn. Grow to give."
–Jordan Paris

Andrew Carnegie led the expansion of the American steel industry in the 19th century. In 1901, he retired, selling his company to J.P. Morgan for a whopping $480 million (which is equivalent to about $14.35 billion in 2017). Carnegie was 66 years old at the time. He could have kept all that money to himself to play with, and he may have felt alright about his overall quality of life by the end of his time. But Carnegie was different. He wanted to become a philanthropist, which he took to the extreme, basically making his full-time occupation *giving away money.* In 1902, he founded a scientific research institution. Then he created a $10 million pension fund for teachers. Since Carnegie was a big believer in reading and learning, his next move was to give money to towns to build over 2,000 public libraries at a time in which America did not have free public libraries. Next, he gave $125 million to schools. Carnegie also believed greatly in world peace, so he established an endowment for international peace and funded a building called The Hague Palace of Peace, which now houses the International Court of Justice. By 1911, just ten years after retirement, it's estimated that he had given away nearly 90 percent of his fortune to charitable causes that meant the most to him. Simply put, the causes of education and peace meant far more to Andrew Carnegie than money ever did. He believed that the sole purpose of making money was to give it all away. In 1919, he passed. I think we should all strive to replicate his model of prosperity: **spend half your life accumulating wealth, then spend the last half giving it all away.** We can all leave this world with prosperity when prosperity doesn't mean monetary riches. **We can leave wealthy and prosperous in terms of love, contribution, and fulfillment.** This is how one of America's most successful and fulfilled human beings lived his life, and I believe it would be a great mistake not to emulate this lifestyle in our own way. Below are some of Mr. Carnegie's most powerful statements:

"No man becomes rich unless he enriches others."
"The man who dies rich, dies disgraced."
"Do real and permanent good in this world."
"Do your duty and a little more and the future will take care of itself."

So, what's the point?

The point is to enrich others, to give value to the world, to uplift others, to empower others, to give like the giving tree and notice the fulfillment in doing just that. **The point of living is to learn, and the point of growing is to give.**

PRINCIPLE 9:

Live to learn. Grow to give.

Chapter Resources: The Giving Tree animated film.

JordanParisHealth.com/gmu-backpack

CHAPTER 10

TOGETHER IS BETTER

"Alone we can do so little; together we can do so much."
—Helen Keller

GROWTH

MINDSET

UNIVERSITY

Ben and Jerry met in a seventh-grade gym class during the early 1960s. They became good friends, and years later they decided to open an ice cream shop affectionately named Ben and Jerry's. With a business fueled by laughs, Ben was the taste-tester, marketer, and scooper while Jerry was primarily the ice cream maker. Together, they made a formidable duo. Separate, Ben and Jerry's as we know it might not exist.

Around the same time, two longtime friends by the name of Steve teamed up to form a company called Apple. Steve Jobs had the vision while Steve Wozniak created the computer. Together, they made a formidable duo. Separate, Apple as we know it might not exist.

A couple of youngsters named Sergey Brin and Larry Page met at Stanford's incoming student orientation. They formed a friendship, and even more with a company called Google. Brin liked data mining while Page was into rankings. Together, they made a formidable duo. Separate, Google as we know it might not exist.

Two well-meaning souls named Marlin and Dory teamed up to search the seas for a fellow named Nemo. Marlin had the smarts while Dory radiated positivity and humor. Together, they formed a formidable duo. Separate, Nemo might still be missing.

Two stepbrothers by the names of Drake and Josh were forced to start living in the same house when their parents got married. Although they were united in some areas (they didn't like their sister Megan), they were different in many others, but they complimented each other well. Together, they formed a funny duo. Separate, kids like me who grew up in the 2000's wouldn't have been graced with such a legendary TV show.

Once upon a time, an ogre named Shrek and a donkey named Donkey set out on a mission to rescue Princess Fiona. Shrek was strong but wasn't good at making friends. Donkey was optimistic and great at making friends. Together, they formed a formidable duo. Separate, Princess Fiona might not have been rescued.

Then there was my friend Chance and I. We set out on a mission to create a podcast that delivered empowering ideas, fresh perspectives, and uplifting conversations for those who seek personal growth. Chance has the fearless confidence and speaking skills while I have the vision of the show and the tech skills. Together, we ... don't form a formidable duo to be honest because we're not all that good *yet*, but eventually we will be. Separate, our podcast might not exist.

And last but certainly not least, SpongeBob and Patrick, my favorite duo, embarked on a mission to find King Neptune's crown and clear Mr. Krabs' name to prevent him from being annihilated by the King. Honestly, SpongeBob and Patrick were both naïve goofballs, but hey, they got the job done. Together, they formed a hilarious duo that shaped mine and many others' childhoods. Separate, Mr. Krabs might not have been saved, and SpongeBob just wouldn't have been that great of a show/movie.

LEVEL UP

"You're an average of the five people you spend the most time with."

—Jim Rohn, and someone in your life at one time or another

Some things in life are tough to do alone. We need friends and partners to help us rise higher in striving to achieve our vision of success.

Many of the formidable duos above had different skill sets than their partners, which makes the formation of these partnerships absolutely genius. Forming these partnerships allowed each individual involved to do something that may not have been able to get done alone. If Steve Jobs didn't have Steve Wozniak, then Apple computers as we know them might not exist.

You see, surrounding ourselves with people who have what we want and believe what we believe (visions aligned) is an easy way to level up in any aspect of our lives we seek to improve. For example, I want to become a better speaker and stop being camera-shy when it comes to video content. Who better to align myself with than a great speaker and totally not camera-shy confident extrovert like my friend Chance? On the flip side, Chance wants to grow and expand his mind. So, who better to align himself with than someone writing a book called *Growth Mindset University.* Not only have we formed a great friendship, but also a strategic partnership in which each of us is leveling up from the unique value we have to offer.

When I wanted to become a personal trainer, I thought it might give me a leg up if I aligned myself with a successful trainer who does exactly what I want to do. Like any 18-year-old high schooler (?), all I did was reach out to a celebrity trainer named Steve Jordan in Los Angeles who has been all over the internet and various magazines, secure a phone call with him, and ask if I could come work for him at his studio in the summer for free by the end of the call. Of course, I had something of value to offer him as well, and that was social media and tech skills. So, he said yes. I went to work for him that summer, and the next summer, and this summer I'm running the studio on my own. Not only have we formed a great friendship, but also a strategic partnership in which each of us is leveling up from the unique value we have to offer.

I wanted to be happier, so I aligned myself with the happiest person I have met and will ever meet in my entire life. His name is Patrick, and he has become my best friend over the past two years. As a result of our time together, I think I became the second happiest person in the world, and I'm still rising in his presence.

> *"If you want to go fast, go alone. If you want to go far, go together."*
> **—African Proverb**

The list could go on, as I've leveraged many relationships so that I can increase my value to the world, but I'll spare you the time. Here's the whole key:

❖ Want to be happy? Surround yourself with happy people.

❖ Want to become a great public speaker? Surround yourself with great public speakers.

❖ Want to stop being so shy? Surround yourself with extroverts.

❖ Want to improve in any area of your life? Surround yourself with people who already have what you want in that area.

Now, proceed with caution because this works in the opposite direction as well; surround yourself with the wrong people, and you will level *down*. If you surround yourself with miserable people, you will inevitably become miserable. If you surround yourself with people who have a fixed mindset, you will inevitably succumb to the poverty of this poor mindset. If you surround yourself with smokers and druggies, you will likely become a smoker and a druggie. If you surround yourself with people who are overweight, you are far more likely to gain weight.

Don't level down, level *up*, my dear friend.

THREE C's

"A dream you dream alone is only a dream. A dream you dream together is reality."

—John Lennon

Together seems to be better. We all need a friend, a partner, some sort of acquaintance to journey down the path of life with us, to share the joy with, to share the love with. I don't know about you, but I value camaraderie, companionship, and connection in my life. I love people, and that love attracts love back in my direction as well, which forms harmonious social relationships. I believe that we are wired to connect in this way, and there is an endless amount of research that backs this belief up.

Balance the Equation

I sure do love my alone time, my Scheduled Me Time. But if my Scheduled Me Time lasted 24 hours per day, 365 days per

141

year, I bet I would be pretty miserable. Not because Scheduled Me Time is a bad thing, but because I would be out of balance. This is why solitary confinement is used as a punishment. The first hour might not be so bad. In fact, it might even be healthy, but it becomes bad when the equation becomes imbalanced. After eight hours of isolation ... eh, I do that sometimes. After 15 hours ... I don't know if I would enjoy that. After three days ... I think that would suck.

By the same token, I think it would also suck to be around others 24 hours per day, 365 days per year. It would be annoying after a while. When my Mother talks about how her and my Father have built such a great relationship over 20 plus years, she often refers to giving each other the chance to *recharge their batteries* as a pillar of the strong love they have endured. What she means by this is that her and my Father have mechanisms built into their relationship that allow for alone time, which provides them with the vital time that is necessary to recharge. This is just one of many ways they make things work. In a world where divorce rates are flying through the roof (last I heard was 53 percent), I seek to model my life and relationships after my parent's.

At one point or another, we must balance the equation. We should spend some time learning, some time with friends, some time alone to recharge and allow ideas to happen, and some time to celebrate your victories. The equation should always be balanced.

You might be wondering the exact amount of time you should be allocating to different aspects of the equation.

To that, I would say *don't think about it too much.* Do what feels right for you, as you please, but ensure that you do not neglect any one aspect. Ensure you are getting some alone time. Ensure you spend time with friends and other people. Ensure you are spending time learning. Ensure you spend time celebrating your victories.

LOVE EVERYONE

"Just go love everybody."
—Bob Goff

I know we already touched on this topic a bit earlier, but I need to mention it again in this chapter because it is crucial.

Have you ever *noticed* how beautiful people are? I mean like really *noticed*, worked up a bit of courage to spark a conversation and ended up getting insight into how their unique perspective shapes their quality of life. It's really freaking cool to see the relationships you can form when you actually talk to people and ask questions out of curiosity instead of staring into your phone screen and not even dignifying the human being next to you. I believe this is something that recent generations struggle mightily with. We're addicted to these stupid black holes that we call smartphones. I call them black holes because we get suckered into scrolling through pointless garbage for multiple hours per day. We are wasting our lives. Worst of all, we're more connected to these black holes than we are to other people, and many of us have no idea how to form meaningful relationships.

I am no exception, but I'm at least aware of what my smartphone is doing to me. This awareness has enabled me to take action ever so slowly. I'm slightly less addicted this year compared to last year. Seeing the relationships that have formed as a result of keeping my phone away has positively reinforced me to stay off my phone when others are around. For example, just this morning (as of this writing) I talked to two outstanding individuals I never would have spoken to had I been staring into my black hole of a smartphone. I've been taking a class with these people for the last three months, but I never made an effort to speak to either one of them (I'm a recovering awkward person). That changed this morning. I sparked a conversation with one lovely lady, making a contextual remark about our surrounding environment. I got a positive response, so I kept talking to her. Over the course of a few hours, we shared many laughs, found out all sorts of things about each other, and gained insights into each other's' unique perspective. I found out some of the things that made her, her. Now, instead of just seeing another person, I see a beautiful soul that has her own dreams, aspirations, drivers, and perspective. Best of all, I made a new friend. I thought that was pretty cool. Next, I found out a guy, who I had previously judged as awkward, has had a wife for two years, a dog, and has a job lined up right out of college. These are just two examples from this morning, but I do this all the time. It allows me to see all humans as uniquely beautiful, even if I don't talk to *every single person,* I know there is beauty in there. And I love people for the beauty in them. Oh, and the side effect to all this is that *people take an interest in you when you are genuinely interested in them.* What a lovely side effect!

"You can make more friends in two months by becoming interested in other people than you can in two years by trying to get other people interested in you."
—Dale Carnegie

PRINCIPLE 10:

If you can do something wonderful with your life (and we all can), then take someone with you.

Chapter Resources: World's biggest eye contact experiment video, the science of human connection TEDx Talk.

JordanParisHealth.com/gmu-backpack

CHAPTER 11

TAKE FULL RESPONSIBILITY

"The man who complains about the way the ball bounces is likely to be the one who dropped it."

—Lou Holtz

GROWTH

MINDSET

UNIVERSITY

I got myself into a fair share of trouble as a child, whether it was being mean to my younger brother or just breaking stuff. I think we all did.

Every single time though, I had an excuse. I had some reason that I believed would justify my actions. I had a long list of things I could blame. But when confronted by my Father, he wouldn't accept my justifications. I would talk back, disagree with him, and go to my Mother saying, "What should I do?"

My Mother would say, "You know he just wants you to take responsibility."

As I grew older, I realized a few things:

1. The confrontations and the problems never went away until I took full responsibility.
2. I would be delusional to think that nothing was my fault.
3. The only thing that should be on my list of things to blame is this: "Me."

Of the many lessons I learned from my Father, this one stands out: **always take full responsibility for your actions and, consequently, your results.** I think that's a good lesson. **We should all take responsibility for our actions, our results, our thoughts, our energy, our mindset, and the order of our entire lives. Own that shit.**

Whether we decide to take responsibility for our lives or

not is the difference between being a winner and being a loser, the difference between success and failure, the difference between living on the track of love and the track of fear, the difference between fulfillment and misery. All of life's glorious riches can be ours if we decide to take responsibility.

"Leaders are the people that take responsibility when things go wrong and give away credit when things go right. Losers are the people who blame when things go wrong and take credit when things go right."
—Jordan Paris

Stock Market Mania

I know a guy named Ted. Ted invests his money in stocks, so do I. There is great power in being able to put your money to work to make more money for you without having to do a thing. However, the market can be volatile at times, and it can be a hazardous place where you might lose your money if you don't know what you're doing. In this case of not having knowledge of the stock market, you're essentially gambling at the casino.

Anyway, whenever Ted makes money from the stocks he has invested in, he always boasts about how great his investment decisions are, as if he's some sort of money wizard where everything he touches turns to gold.

Whenever Ted loses money, though, from the stocks he has invested in, he always points to the market being bad. It is always the market's poor state as the reason he loses money.

This is just plain silly though. Quite frankly, this is the mindset of the losers, the ones who fail to take responsibility for all of their results.

You see, we can't just decide to take responsibility for *some* of our results. **We can't take responsibility only when we win** and deflect responsibility when we lose. This is a flawed way of thinking. It's all well and good to take responsibility when we win, but we must ensure to do the same when we lose.

"The price of greatness is responsibility."
—Winston Churchill

PRINCIPLE 11:

Take responsibility, give away credit.

CHAPTER 12

LIVE IMPACTFULLY

"In a gentle way, you can shake the world."
—Mahatma Gandhi

GROWTH

MINDSET

UNIVERSITY

IMPACT.

Many dream of it, few know what it means, and even fewer end up making a real impact. Everyone says, "I want to make an impact." But what does that even mean? It's this big concept that we all talk about, maybe because it sounds impressive or whatever, but very few of us have any clue about precisely how we are going to make an impact. "I'm going to change the world" is the next thing we'll say. More empty words.

Here's my take on making an impact: Think small. I'm all about thinking big in most areas of life. After all, **when we look back on our lives, we won't be thankful that we played it small. Rather, we'll be thankful that we went for it all, took the necessary calculated risks, and that we did all that we could.** But doing all that we can doesn't always mean that we must think big. In fact, **we should be thinking *small* in terms of making an impact because many of us overestimate the impact we can make on the world but underestimate the impact we can make on the people that are close to us, our friends, our community, and our children. Somehow, we overlook the people already near and dear to us and our own ability to influence them along their respective journeys.** In this chapter, we will delve into how each of us can make a real, lasting impact.

EIGHT WAYS TO MAKE AN IMPACT

#1 – Leave Your Knowledge Behind

My 15-year-old client Brett is right on with his idea of building a library. I'm in the process of building mine. We should all build a library.

But why?

Very simple. Because **building a library to leave behind for your own children and future generations is the single most excellent way to make an impact and have your legacy carried on.** A library is the most valuable thing someone can inherit because it's not just books that are being inherited; knowledge is being inherited, thought patterns are being inherited, empowering ideas are being inherited, fresh perspectives are being inherited, philosophy is being inherited, strong character is being inherited. **What better to leave behind than the very thing that taught you and formed your philosophy?**

What a gift.

"A library outranks any other one thing a community can do to benefit its people. It is a never-failing spring in the desert."
—Andrew Carnegie

#2 – Leave Your Ideas Behind

We should leave behind our unique perspectives, ideas, and knowledge nuggets that we have crafted over the years in the form of a journal, the notes about all that we've learned over a lifetime. **Hear something impactful? Write it down. Read something impactful? Write that down too. Let it all accumulate into equities and values of all kind, not just for you, but for the person you pass these journals down to.**

How powerful.

*"No matter what people tell you, words and ideas can change
the world."*
—Robin Williams

#3 – Document Your Life

Books and journals are great. They have many words in them.
But **one picture can tell 1,000 words. They give insight into
your perspective, your lens through which you see the world.**
There is immense power in pictures, so it's crucial that we
document our lives by taking these pictures so that someone
from future generations can look at them and gain some
insight.

No, I'm not talking about social media posts and dog-
filtered Snapchat selfies. That's not what we're going for here.
Instead, take pictures of your friends, with your friends, events
you go to, nature, your sister trying to get spaghetti in her
mouth, your car, your family, funny stuff, and whatever else
your heart desires. Then put them in a little photo album. It
might sound a bit old-fashioned, but I don't think this is
something that should ever go away because I don't have much
faith in social media and technology's reliability:

1. Hard drives crash.

2. I doubt cloud-based storage services are going to keep
   our files for eternity when we die and stop paying.

3. Nobody will be looking at your Facebook albums in
   50-100 years (or less) because who knows where
   Facebook will be.

4. Nobody will be scrolling through your Instagram feed
   in 50-100 years (or less) because, again, who knows
   where Instagram will be. Plus, **Instagram feeds rarely**

portray the truth of our lives. The pictures might still tell 1,000 words, but they probably aren't the right words.

5. Nobody can access your Snapchat memories but you. Plus, I think it would be pretty damn weird if your children showed their children a picture of you, said "look, it's grandma," and have it be a picture of you with animated dog ears, a dog nose, and a dog tongue. I don't know about that one.

#4 – Teach People How to Think

This is very different than merely telling people what to do. That doesn't influence anybody. Nobody wants to be told what to do.

Share your perspective. Challenge people to rise higher with new levels of thinking so that they can reach new levels of their destiny. Challenge them to get out of the boat if they want to walk on water, to get out of their comfort zone if they want to achieve anything in life. **Ask them questions that can profoundly influence the way they think.**

- ❖ What level of thinking would it take for you to achieve _____?
- ❖ What do you think (insert their hero here) would do in this situation?

#5 – Uplift Others

In every interaction, make it your personal goal to leave each person feeling uplifted. Leave on a high note, because people are more likely to remember the most recent thing, which is known as the recency effect in psychology circles. This is why movies and books aim to end on high notes. It's also why when our friends cancel on us, we then turn around and say, "they do that all the time" even though it only happened that one time. The bottom line is this: **The last, most recent thing is what holds the most value in the minds of others. Now, Imagine the influence and impact you would have if you made sure you left everyone you came into contact with feeling uplifted.** Plus, people will always remember how you made them feel, not necessarily what you said.

#6 – Hold Up the Mirror for Others

Whether it is for better or worse, we need more people that hold up mirrors for others in this world. We're not as self-aware as we think, so I believe it to be vitally important that we hold up mirrors for others, letting them know the path they seem to be on, the person they seem to be becoming, even if it isn't something they want to hear. Because sometimes people must look in the mirror and see what they don't want to see to end up becoming who they really want to become. On the flip side, if you notice the seeds of greatness blooming within someone, tell that person. It's another chance to uplift.

#7 – Plant Seeds of Greatness in Others

Planting seeds of greatness in others is one of the greatest ways we can serve others and make an impact. Oh, and it's super easy. Here are four simple ways we can plant these seeds:

- ❖ **Gift someone with a book you enjoyed and extracted a ton of value from.** I always say that a book is one of the best gifts you can give to someone, whether they read it now, in two months, or in two years, it could change his or her life, and it shows you to be a person of good taste and generosity.

❖ **Recommend a book to someone.** Often, when I'm engaged in conversation with someone, I pick up on context clues that help me to identify which areas of their life they want to improve. Once I've identified the area in which they seek improvement, I recommend a corresponding book that I've read that will help them in that area. Honestly, this is incredibly natural for me. It's a practice that has been drilled into my subconscious mind. At the same time, I'm not a total self-improvement junkie that recommends books to every person I talk to. That would be weird. It is hard for me to articulate the exact type of person and conversation that triggers a book recommendation because it's this feeling I get in my limbic brain (region of the brain responsible for emotions and has no capacity for language) when I'm engaged in conversation that gives me the inclination to help this person, which for me manifests itself in the form of a book recommendation and uplifting words. I would say I do this about two or three times per week. For this, go with your gut.

❖ **Send a podcast to someone.** If you hear a podcast that offered a lot of value or moved you in any way, don't just keep it to yourself, share it with a friend that might also relate to the message. Text it to someone, email it to someone, put it on your Instagram story, share it to Facebook.

❖ **Be a highlighter.** When interacting with someone, highlight what makes them unique, their skills, or what you like about that them. Uplift them, hold up the mirror for them. This will make you more likable as well because humans like people who like them.

If you execute these impact practices (impractices?), don't be surprised to hear "That conversation you and I had that day changed my life," or "You and I had that conversation way back when and I've been on track ever since," or "I read that book you said I should get, and it changed my life." You may not receive these tokens of appreciation the next day, the next month, or even in the year following these valuable conversations. In some cases, you'll never hear it because the person wasn't open to new ideas and perspectives. There's nothing more you can do. You can lead them to water, but ultimately, they have to drink. But **you never know the difference a few words can make. Let me tell you, sometimes you plant those seeds, like small investments that cost you nothing, and they absolutely bloom, bringing forth sweet fruit. This is real impact.**

#8 – Write a Book

Gosh, I can't wait for my children and the future generations of my family to read this book, just because there's a chance it may make a difference in their lives. It may steer them in the right direction. It may encourage them to seek what is true for them. It may add a new perspective for them.

Even if one person reads your book, I'd call that a success. I didn't write this book for 20 million people to read it, I wrote this book so that *someone somewhere* could get *something* of value from it. If one person felt empowered and compelled to take control of his or her life because of this book, then I'll be ecstatic. That would do it for me. That's powerful stuff. That's real impact. And in the same way that I believe everybody can and should run a blog, **I believe everyone can and should write a book. Every single person has a unique perspective, a unique lens through which he or she sees the world. We all have some sort of book-worthy value that someone in the world can** extract value from.

METRICS

If we want to feel fulfilled by making an "impact," we should clearly define the metrics we're going to use to measure this "impact." In this way, we can turn an abstract concept into something very real and very attainable. For example, only one person has to read my book for me to feel like I made an impact. This is my metric that measures whether I made an impact or not. So, when one person reads my book, I'll be delighted. And since you're currently reading these words, you've checked that box for me, you've made me feel like I made an impact. Thank you.

Now, imagine if I had it made up in my mind that 20 million people had to read my book before I felt like I made an impact. I would probably be miserable for eternity! This is a poor metric to measure impact with. With poor metrics, you could be winning at life while simultaneously *feeling* like you are losing just because the method by which you keep score is unfair.

So, let's stop making this impact thing so complicated. Clearly define the metrics by which you are going to measure your impact below, either by filling in the blanks or by writing a similar statement:

I will feel like I have made an impact when I do _____ (thing/accomplishment) for ____ (#) person/people.

LIVE ON

Steve Jordan, one of my mentors, was a difference maker in my life. He uplifted me when I was a bit lost in life just after high school. He served as the bridge that lead me from a time of trouble to a time of triumph. He taught me how to think, how to act, how to speak, and even how to stand with confidence. He planted seeds of greatness in me; sharing podcasts, books, and other great things with me. He consistently held up the mirror for me to see what I was becoming, highlighting the good in me, and telling me of the prosperities I would attain with this good I already possessed. Steve *saw* me in a way that nobody had ever seen me before. **I think that's what most of us want in life, to be seen, to be understood and believed in, especially when we feel broken.** Steve did that for me. Then, I started to believe wholeheartedly in the declarations he made over my career and my life, and it made them come true. Whether Steve knows it or not, he's made a profound impact on me, and for this reason, his thought patterns, his ideas, his uplifting words, his philosophy, his work ethic, his lessons, and all else that he passed down to me will live on, continually shining through in my life as a beacon of light that attracts people, so that I can share his impact further.

My Uncle Brian was another difference maker in my life. Brian's approach was similar to Steve's; he uplifted me, he taught me how to think, he recommended and gifted me with books (many of which I did not read for years), he shared podcasts with me, and he challenged me to no end to rise higher. Brian made a profound impact on me, and for this reason, his thought patterns, his ideas, his uplifting words, his philosophy, his work ethic, his lessons, and all else that he passed down to me will live on, continually shining through in my life as a beacon of light that attracts people, so that I can share his impact further.

My Father's lessons in personal responsibility will live on through me. My Mother's love for people will also live on through me. There have been many individuals that have made an impact on me, and their gifts will live on through my own life.

My friend, with the impact you make, you can live impactfully through someone else long after you've passed. Your philosophy, your ideas, your uplifting words, your wisdom, your perspective can shine through in someone else's life, and they can pass it down to the next person, and the next person. You can live on. You just have to share a little bit.

PRINCIPLE 12:

To make an impact, define impact, then make it happen.

Chapter Resources: Meet Steve Jordan, how to write your book in 29 days.

JordanParisHealth.com/gmu-backpack

NOTES FROM A FRIEND

Dear friend,

It is my sincere desire that the joy I experienced while relentlessly writing this book over the past 29 days shined through on every page, and I hope that light uplifted your mind and brightened your spirit. I hope you felt the eternal purpose that drove my inspiration to write this book. I hope you realize that you, your relationships, your situation, and the order of your entire life never have to be the same again, only by choice. I hope your eyes have been opened to new possibilities, and that you will explore these wonderfully fantastic possibilities. I hope seeds of greatness have been planted in you, and that you will decide to continually water these seeds. I hope you have been moved in a way that you are purposefully compelled to creatively and effectively design your life. I hope you are inspired to seek your own truth. Most of all, I hope you are inspired to perpetually optimize the order of your entire life.

Now, I know this a lot of hoping from someone that chastises the act, but the most I can do is plant seeds of greatness in you; ultimately, it is your choice whether you water them or not. I've done everything I can do to plant these seeds, but the ball is in your court now.

As you continue to explore and seek new possibilities for your life, you may stumble upon books that support my principles.

You will also find books that oppose my principles. But none of that matters, because this is just what's true for me at the moment, and you should seek what's true for you. No one book or person will give us all the answers.

This final chapter serves as a collection of things to keep in mind as you journey through life. Think of this like notes from a friend, your friend Jordan. I know the journey is tough sometimes, so if you ever need help or just want to talk or say hello, I'll be there for you. Email me anytime at Jordan@JordanParisHealth.com, and I'll give you my undivided attention.

Speaking of your life's journey, I think this is important to keep at the forefront of your thoughts:
Life is not a sprint. It's not a marathon. It's not even a race at all.
Life is a process. It's a journey. It's a path.
Whether we travel it quickly or slowly, we must ensure we stop to appreciate all things good, all things bad, and trust the process of it all.

Here's something I believe to be true: You can build any skill and accomplish anything you want with consistent effort. We may be born with different skill sets, but everything is trainable and everything is attainable in the end, which means you can be who you want to be and do what you want to do. I'm sure you know that though. I trust you will harness this great power to be found in continual growth and development to become all you were created to be.

With LOVE always,

Your friend, Jordan.

BEWARE OF THE TRAP

"There is nothing noble in being superior to your fellow man; true nobility is being superior to your former self."
—Ernest Hemingway

Once we think we know it all, we've peaked. Once we think we're better than others, we've peaked. Once we think our problems are more important than others', we've peaked. Once we think we are larger than life itself, we've peaked. A steady decline follows this peak, no matter who you are.

THE GATEWAY VIRTUE: HUMILITY

"A true genius admits that he/she knows nothing."
—Albert Einstein

To ensure you do not fall prey to the trap of knowing it all, we must always stay humble. We must understand that we will always be students of life. We must understand that we are never too important for certain people, that we are never larger than life, that we are not the best and never will be. No matter how much we've accomplished, we should always feel like we are just getting started. This humility breeds wisdom, excellence, success, wealth, discipline, gratitude, creativity, service, and prosperities of all kind. Humility is the gateway virtue that leads to all good things in life.

LIFE BEAUTIFULLY DESIGNED

We all have different ideas of what a beautifully designed life looks like. For me, life beautifully designed is full of love, laughter, learning, growth, and giving. What does life beautifully designed look like for you?

JOY, *NOW*

"Success does not lead to happiness; instead, happiness leads to success."

—Chade-Meng Tan

Yes, there is a lot to learn, there is a ton to achieve, and there is an endless amount of room for growth. But that doesn't mean we can't be happy right now. Don't fall prey to the trap "I'll be happy when I get/do _____."

Years ago, I was waiting to be happy. I thought "I'll be happy when I get this Porsche."

Here are my thoughts on that now: fuck that!

I realized I would probably be happy for all of five minutes anyway if I went and bought it, and I would soon return to my previous level of happiness.

It might sound cheesy, but if we can appreciate and notice the things we already have, the people in our lives, the things we have gone through, the little things in our day, the opportunity we have, the breathe that fills our lungs, the adventure in a smile, then we can live joyfully *today*. No need to wait. Let's meditate on these things, and notice the joy in them.

If we can learn to strive and grow joyfully, we're in for a good, balanced life.

THE PRINCIPLES

Principle 1: Adopt a growth mindset and drop limiting beliefs.

Principle 2: Feed the mind or fall behind.

Principle 3: Develop your purpose.

Principle 4: Work harder on yourself than anything else.

Principle 5: For an extraordinary quality of life, ask an extraordinary quality of questions.

Principle 6: Start viewing setbacks as setups and trouble as transportation.

Principle 7: Forget what others think and get after your dreams today.

Principle 8: Don't go with the flow, direct the flow; Don't make a living, design a life.

Principle 9: Live to learn. Grow to give.

Principle 10: If you have the opportunity to do something wonderful with your life, then take someone with you.

Principle 11: Take responsibility, give away credit.

Principle 12: To make an impact, define impact, then make it happen.

JORDAN'S LAWS

Law of Accumulated Prosperity: The result of consistently investing in one's self is a prosperous life, and it's those consistent acts that matter more than any one act of intensity.

Law of Accuracy: We are all wrong.

Law of Wisdom: Since we are all wrong and there is an infinite number of things that can be true for any given person, the only path to wisdom is an accumulation of different perspectives.

Law of Infinite Truths: Two opposing statements can be true for different people. Therefore, all statements can be true.

Law of Confidence: To develop confidence, we must develop ourselves.

EQUATIONS

- ❖ Clarity of vision = Excitement and a prosperous life
- ❖ No vision = No excitement and no prosperity
- ❖ Quality questions = Quality answers and a quality life
- ❖ Poor quality questions = Poor quality answers and a poor quality life
- ❖ Problems = Progress
- ❖ Time learning + time celebrating + time with friends + time alone = A balanced life
- ❖ Backloaded stress = A mess
- ❖ Frontloaded stress = Success

"Live as if you were to die tomorrow. Learn as if you were to live forever."

—Mahatma Gandhi

ABOUT THE AUTHOR

JORDAN PARIS, born September 29, 1997, is an entrepreneur, web developer, author, podcast host, former college-athlete, and personal trainer showcased in Men's Health as a beacon of light for inspiring people from all walks of life. His online coaching is sought-after by people across the globe.

You can visit him at JordanParisHealth.com.

ACKNOWLEDGEMENTS

Thank you to my wonderfully fantastic family, as I've been blessed to be a part of such a tight-knit, loving family. Without them, none of this would be possible. Thank you to my father, Scot, for teaching me always to take full responsibility. Thank you to my mother, Maria, for showing me the beauty inside others even though I never believed any of it as you consoled me crying in my room all those times. Everybody says they have the best parents, but I know, and everyone who has met my parents knows that I truly do have the best parents. Thanks for raising me with such care even though I was the most challenging child. Thanks for always giving me the freedom to make my own choices and for encouraging me to run down my dreams. I am eternally grateful for the unconditional love and support each of you bestows upon my siblings and me. Thank you to my brother, Devon, for being my competitor in sports for almost two decades now, even though I have to let you win sometimes! Thank you to my sister, Tiffany, for allowing me to get my built-up jokes out of my system and for always laughing at them. Thank you to all of my grandparents, for raising such amazing parents and for being my role models. Thank you to my Uncle Brian for being my first real coach/teacher/mentor. You continually planted priceless seeds of greatness within me, even though it took me many years to get to water them, so thanks for not giving up on me. I'm not sure if any of this would be possible without your guidance. Oh, and thanks for always crushing me with your workouts. Thank you to my Uncle Jay for teaching me to eat right and also for planting seeds of greatness in me.

Thank you to my mentor and friend, Steve Jordan, for understanding and believing in me when nobody else did, including myself. Thank you for accepting that first internship request, as I probably would have wasted away working at some crappy gym otherwise. Thank you for continually teaching me, reassuring me, and guiding me when I am in need.

To the one friend I had in high school, Peter, thank you for sticking by my side and always being up to go play basketball, baseball, or football because those were the best memories I have of that 4 year period. I don't know what I would have done without you.

Thank you to my friend Patrick, for always being there to talk to and for being my personal guidance counselor. Thank you for the constant love and support. Thank you for the book of reminders you penned for me to keep on my bedside table. In tough times, this book has been invaluable. Thank you for helping me navigate through the various complexities of the college life. Most of all, thanks for teaching me the art of communication.

Thank you to the teachers that have instructed me from afar: Tony Robbins, Simon Sinek, Brendon Burchard, Tim Tebow, Tim Ferriss, Don Miguel Ruiz, Joel Osteen, Jim Rohn, Malcolm Gladwell, Vanessa Van Edwards, Jim Kwik, Chade-Meng Tan, Paul Chek, Lewis Howes, Mark Manson, and many more.

Thank you to every teacher I ever had at Spring-Ford, especially those who taught me my favorite subject, Spanish! Thanks for teaching me to be a hard-worker.

Thank you to anyone who has ever bestowed kind words upon me, I don't forget these deeds.

Thank you to my clients. You are the lights of my life.

Thank you to my readers for your generous attention and comments.

Thank you to all of my friends for supporting me even when I shelter myself to work on a project for months at a time. I know I have a bit of a bad habit in the way I isolate myself until a project is completed, but I want you to know that you were in my heart with each passing page. Life would be meaningless without you all, so thank you very much.

REFERENCES

Chapter 1: THE GROWTH MINDSET

1. Bauer, Jack J, et al. "Growth Motivation Toward Two Paths of Eudaimonic Self-Development." Journal of Happiness Studies, vol. 16, no. 1, Feb. 2015, p. 185. ProQuest, doi:10.1007/s10902-014-9504-9.

2. Zawadzka, Anna Maria, and Anna Szabowska-Walaszczyk. "Does Self-Improvement Explain Well-Being in Life and at Workplace? Analysis Based on Selected Measures of Well-Being." Polish Psychological Bulletin, vol. 45, no. 2, 2014, p. 134. ProQuest, doi:10.2478/ppb-2014-0018.

3. Moldovan, Ramona, et al. "Cognitive Bibliotherapy for Mild Depressive Symptomatology: Randomized Clinical Trial of Efficacy and Mechanisms of Change." Clinical Psychology & Psychotherapy, Nov. 2013. ProQuest, search.proquest.com/docview/1492643643.

4. Bergsma, Ad. "Do Self-Help Books Help?" Journal of Happiness Studies, vol. 9, no. 3, Sept. 2008, p. 341. ProQuest, doi:10.1007/s10902-006-9041-2.

5. Bergsma, Ad. "The Advice of the Wise." Journal of Happiness Studies, vol. 9, no. 3, Sept. 2008, p. 331. ProQuest, doi:10.1007/s10902-006-9040-3.

6. Kane, Libby. "What Rich People Have Next To Their Beds." Business Insider, Business Insider, 17 June 2014, www.businessinsider.com/rich-people-read-self-improvement-books-2014-6.Business Insider, Business Insider, 17 June 2014, www.businessinsider.com/rich-people-read-self-improvement-books-2014-6.

7. Schocker, Laura. "6 Science-Backed Reasons To Go

Read A Book Right Now." The Huffington Post, TheHuffingtonPost.com, 7 Dec. 2017, www.huffingtonpost.com/2015/08/05/health-benefits-reading_n_4081258.html.

8. Claro, Susana, et al. "Growth Mindset Tempers the Effects of Poverty on Academic Achievement." PNAS, National Academy of Sciences, 2 Aug. 2016, www.pnas.org/content/113/31/8664.full.